John D. McFaden

The Bible Reader's Assistant

John D. McFaden

The Bible Reader's Assistant

ISBN/EAN: 9783337171858

Printed in Europe, USA, Canada, Australia, Japan

Cover: Foto ©Lupo / pixelio.de

More available books at **www.hansebooks.com**

THE

BIBLE READER'S ASSISTANT.

CONTAINS

THE CORRECT PRONUNCIATION OF BIBLE PROPER
NAMES, AND OTHER VALUABLE FEATURES.

———

"SEARCH THE SCRIPTURES."

———

AN ASSISTANT TO MINISTERS, CHURCH MEMBERS, SCHOOL TEACH-
ERS, SUNDAY-SCHOOL SCHOLARS, AND ALL PERSONS
WHO READ THE BIBLE.

———

THE BRETHREN TRACT SOCIETY,
PHILADELPHIA, PA.
1887.

PREFACE.

The Bible-Reader's Assistant has been compiled for the purpose of assisting Ministers, Church-Members, Sunday-school Teachers, Sunday-school Scholars, and all persons who use the Bible.

The word Bible—The word Testament—The word Gospel—The word Selah—Figurative Language of the Bible—Sects mentioned in the Bible—Hebrew Officers referred to in the Bible—The Origin of Nations, etc., contain reference and other valuable information useful and convenient.

The miracles of Christ—The Parables of Christ—The Discourses of Christ, etc., arranged with references to book, chapter, and verse, will prove useful to many. Often you wish to refer to some miracle, parable, or discourse of Christ, but cannot remember the place; here as in other points you will find the book an assistant.

The List of Bible Proper Names and their Correct Pronunciation needs only to be used to be appreciated. Men stop to sneeze when they suddenly run against such words as *Apharsathchites* or *Bashan-havoth-jair;* they mutilate the Scripture by leaving out the "hard words," and it loses force. You need not be afraid to read any verse with this book at hand. The word is in one column, and just opposite is its correct pronunciation. At a glance confusion dissolves into harmony.

If you find errors, report them. If you have something good for the next edition, send it to me. What has helped you will help others. In the words of Bickersteth : " Reader, join in praying that it may please the great *Head of the Church* to bless this, and every attempt, to lead men to the study of that Book, which is so peculiarly *His Own.*"

JOHN DUKE MCFADEN.

2720 N. 8th street,
PHILADELPHIA, PA.

(3)

Israel, in ancient days,
Not only had a view
Of Sinai in a blaze,
But learn'd the gospel too;
The types and figures were a glass,
In which they saw a Saviour's face.

The paschal sacrifice,
And blood-besprinkled door,
Seen with enlightened eyes,
And once applied with power,
Would teach the need of other blood,
To reconcile the world to God.

The lamb, the dove set forth
His perfect innocence,
Whose blood of matchless worth
Should be the soul's defence,
For he, who can for sin atone,
Must have no failing of his own.

The scapegoat on his head
The people's trespass bore,
And, to the desert led,
Was to be seen no more;
In him, our surety seem'd to say,
Behold, I bear your sins away.

Dipt in his fellow's blood,
The living bird went free;
The type well understood,
Express'd the sinner's plea;
Describ'd a guilty soul enlarged,
And by a Saviour's death discharg'd.

Jesus, I love to trace,
Throughout the sacred page,
The footsteps of thy grace,
The same in every age.
Oh, grant that I may faithful be
To clearer light, vouchsaf'd to me.

—Cowper.

(4)

THE BIBLE-READER'S ASSISTANT.

THE WORD BIBLE.

The word "BIBLE" signifies *Book*, and is so called on account of its being a Book of Books, sixty-six in all. The whole Bible, consisting of the Old and New Testaments, is commonly called the "SCRIPTURES," a word which signifies *writings*. They were written by different persons, at different times and in different places, and since the canon of Scripture has been filled up, as also before, the whole is called "*The book of the Lord:*" Isa. xxxiv. 16. They were inspired by the Lord, and abound with the most sublime descriptions of him, 2 Tim. iii. 16, 17. The Bible describes not only the nature of God and what He is in himself, but also the relations in which he stands to us as his creatures, Isa. lxiii. 16; Mal. ii. 10. And scarcely could there be a question asked, by any serious mind, concerning the Divine Being, but may be answered by the Scriptures. They are sanctioned by the Lord, and he has affixed his seal to the truth of them. See Isa. lv. 10, 11; Rom. i. 16; 1 Thess. ii. 13. They find us far from God, and mark out the path by which we are brought back to our Father's house, Isa. liii. 6; John iii. 16–18. If you would gain *instruction*, attentively read the Bible, for that is a book of knowledge, with every page replete with sacred information, 2 Tim. iii. 15. If you want *examples*, you will find the Bible a book of models, for the precepts there contained not only describe what men ought to be, but, in living characters, show what they really were, Heb. xi. To gain *excitements* you have only to read the Bible, and you have a book of motives the most powerful, addressed, not only to the understanding, but to the conscience and heart. If you need *encouragements*, all you have to do is to read your Bible, for there you have a book of " precious promises " and " strong consolations," suited to every case, and well calculated to meet every emergency, Ps. xix. 7–11.

THE WORD TESTAMENT.

The word " TESTAMENT " signifies the will of a dying man left in writing, by which he determines how his property shall be disposed of after his death, Gal. iii. 15. And the TESTATOR is the deceased person who left the *testament*, or *will*. JESUS CHRIST is called a TESTATOR, on account of his having bequeathed to sinful men his peace, John xiv. 27, together with all the unsearchable riches of his grace and glory, Heb. ix. 16, 17. The writings of Moses and the prophets are called the *Old Testament*, and this *testament*, or *will*, was published before the birth of the Redeemer. Notwithstanding, it was ratified by his typical death in the many sacrifices that were offered, which observances are now entirely abolished or done away. See 2 Cor. iii. 14; Heb. ix. 15.

The writings of the *Evangelists* and *Apostles* are called the NEW TESTAMENT, and may be considered the voluntary *act* and *deed* of JESUS CHRIST, duly executed and witnessed, bestowing legacies on such characters as he has described, and, being ratified by the death of the Testator, can never be abolished. The *New* Testament is the same in substance with the *Old*, but is more spiritual, clear, efficacious and extensive. The wine in the Lord's Supper is called the " *new testament* in Christ's blood," Matt. xxvi. 28, because it represents the blood which sealed the covenant God has been pleased to make with his creatures, and all the benefits and privileges of it are owing to the merits of that blood, represented by the wine, Luke xxii. 20. The *Old* Testament was confirmed by the blood of bulls and of goats, Ex. xxiv. 8, but the *New* with the blood of Christ, without the shedding of which our sins could never have been removed, nor heaven have become our inheritance, Heb. ix. 22.

The word we have rendered *Testament* might well be rendered *Covenant*, for it signifies both; and so it would read *New Covenant*. But in speaking of Christ's act and deed it is most proper to render it *Testament*, for he is the *Testator*, and by his death it became in force, Heb. ix. 16, 17. There is nothing in the Old Testament laid aside by the New Testament but the ceremonial law and peculiarities of the Jews.

THE WORD GOSPEL.

The word " GOSPEL " signifies *good news* or *glad tidings*, as it exhibits the covenant of grace, and is an absolute declaration of the good-will of God to man in freely giving Jesus Christ and salvation in him, to be received by the vilest, without money and without price. See Luke ii. 10, 11; Mark xvi. 15. It is called the *Gospel of God*, on account of its originally coming from him, Rom. i. 1. It is called the *Gospel of the grace of God*, because it comes from and makes known to us the favor of God, and is the channel through which his grace is conveyed to us, Acts xx. 24. It is called the *Gospel of Christ*, because he is the Author and subject-matter of it, Rom. i. 16. It is called the *Gospel of salvation*, because it not only tells us that salvation may be had, but points out the way of obtaining, and offers it to us, Eph. i. 13. It is the same gospel that the Spirit of God preached unto Abraham. See Gal. iii. 8; Gen. xii. 3; xviii. 18; xxii.

18; **xxvi. 4.** *Gospel* is also taken for a historical account of what Jesus Christ did and said; of his life, doctrines, miracles, sufferings, death, resurrection and ascension; hence we say, "the Gospel according to Matthew," or Mark, or Luke, or John. That is, as recorded by them. See Mark i. 1.

THE WORD SELAH.

The translators of the Bible have left the Hebrew word *Selah*, which occurs so often in the Psalms, as they found it; and, of course, the reader often asks his minister what it means. And he has often been obliged to confess his ignorance, because it is a matter in regard to which the most learned have by no means been of one mind. The Targums and most of the Jewish commentators give to the word the meaning of *eternally, forever.* Rabbi Kimchi regards it as a sign to elevate the voice. The authors of the Septuagint translation appear to have regarded it as a musical or rhythmical note. Herder regards it as indicating a change of tone. Matheson thinks it, as a musical note, equivalent, perhaps, to the word *repeat.* According to Luther and others, it means *silence.* Gesenius explains it to mean: "Let the instruments play and the singers stop!" Woecher regards it as equivalent to *Sursum corda*—"Up! my soul!" Sommer, after examining all the seventy-four passages in which the word occurs, recognizes in every case "an actual appeal or summons to Jehovah. They are calls for aid and prayers to be heard, expressed either with entire directness, or, if not in the imperative, 'Hear, Jehovah!' or 'Awake, Jehovah!' and the like, still earnest addresses to God that he would remember and hear," etc. The word itself he regards as indicating a blast of trumpets by the priests. Selah, itself, he thinks an abridged expression used for Higgaion Selah—Higgaion indicating the sound of the stringed instruments, and Selah a vigorous blast of trumpets.

(9)

ANALYSIS OF THE BIBLE.

The following table is believed to contain accurate particulars of the English version of the Bible; and though it may profit but few, it will probable please most readers of the book.

	In the Old Testament.	In the New Testament.	Total.
Books	39	27	66
Chapters	929	260	1,189
Verses	23,214	7,959	31,173
Words	592,493	181,253	773,746
Letters	2,728,100	838,380	3,566,480

The middle chapter, and the shortest in the Bible, is the one hundred and seventeenth Psalm, the middle verse is the eighth of the one hundred and eighteenth Psalm. The nineteenth chapter of the second book of Kings and the thirty-seventh chapter of the book of Isaiah are alike. The twenty-first verse of the seventh chapter of Ezra has all the letters of the alphabet in it, excepting J. The word *and* occurs in the Old Testament 35,543 times, in the New Testament 10,684. The word *Jehovah* occurs 6,855 times.

SOMETHING TO REMEMBER.

In the New Testament, it frequently occurs that *names* are differently spelt from what they are in the Old. For example, Isaiah is called *Esaias:* Matt. iii. 3; Isa. xl. 3, 4. Joshua, who was a type of the Redeemer, is, according to the true signification of his name, called *Jesus:* Acts. vii. 45; Heb. iv. 8. Hosea is called *Osee:* Rom. ix. 25; Hosea i. 10; ii. 23. This should ever be kept in mind, or we may make many serious mistakes in reading. To properly understand the true meaning of any passage, or chapter, it will be well to consider the whole design of the writer; and this will be readily discovered by the preceding and following parts of the same book.

How to Read the Bible Through in a Year.

The following plan is old, and no doubt familiar to the reader, but it is worthy of a place here. It can be easily referred to, and may act as a guide to some other plan.

Read three chapters on week-days and five on the Sabbath : that is, two chapters in the Old Testament daily and on week-days one chapter in Psalms, Proverbs, Ecclesiastes, Solomon's Song, or the New Testament—three on the Sabbath.

The Old Testament, without these four books, contains two chapters a day for the year ; and the New Testament, with the four books, has one chapter a day, and three for Sabbath days, *less* eight chapters.

Read Psalm cxix., as eleven chapters of two divisions each, and connect the short Psalms cxvii. and cxxxi. with the next, and cxxxiii. and cxxxiv. together—thus adding eight chapters to complete the year.

Figurative Language of the Bible.

The Bible abounds with figures drawn from nature, persons and the church. The Bible itself is the best guide to the interpretation of its own figures—as the Epistle to the Hebrews to the ceremonial law.

You will find the following to be the most remarkable figures of speech in the Bible, and by making yourself acquainted with them you will find a key to unlock an invaluable treasure.

A Metaphor is a word applied to some use to which, in its literal meaning, it could not be put ; but is founded on the similitude one object bears to another : such as, " For the *sword* to devour flesh," Deut. xxxii. 42.

An Allegory is a metaphor continued : as the Saviour's discourse concerning the eating of his own flesh : " I am the *bread* of life," etc., John vi. 35-65.

A Parable is a similitude, and illustrates something we do not known by a statement of something we are familiar with, and is used to impress it more deeply on the mind: as, the Lost Sheep, the Prodigal Son, etc., Luke xv.

A Proverb is a short, energetic sentence, containing great meaning in a few words ; and a wise man will understand them. The requisites of a proverb are elegance and brevity : Prov. i. 1–6 ; x. 15 Luke iv. 23.

A Metonymy is a figure of speech in which one word is put for another : as, " They have Moses and the prophets," meaning their writings and not their persons : Luke xvi. 29.

A Prosopopœia, or *personification*, is a figure by which *things* are spoken of as *persons :* as, " *Mercy* and *truth* are met together; *righteousness* and *peace* have kissed each other : " Ps. lxxxv. 10.

A Synecdoche is a figure by which the whole is put for a part of anything, or a part for the whole ; as, "*All the world should be taxed ;* " when no more is meant than the Roman empire : Luke ii. 1. "And we were in all, in the ship, two hundred threescore and sixteen *souls ;* " when persons, *bodies* and souls, are intended.

Irony is a figurative form of speech, in which the meaning is contrary to what is spoken, and though there are not many examples of the kind in the Bible, there are some few : such as Elijah's address to the prophets of Baal, 2 Kings xviii. 27; and Job's remark to his friends, Job xii. 2. Though a different thing is meant from what is spoken, *irony* may readily be understood. If a father should say to his son, who had disobeyed him, " *You* are a good lad ! " —the son would well understand his father to mean that *he* was a *bad lad*.

A Hyperbole is a figure by which anything is represented as being much greater, or smaller, than it really is ; examples of which you will find recorded in the following passages : Numb. xiii. 33; Deut. i. 28; John xxi. 25.

SECTS MENTIONED IN THE BIBLE.

The Samaritans were the descendants of those idolatrous nations whom the king of Assyria sent to unite with the scattered few, in peopling Samaria and the land of Israel. They established a system of religion compounded of Judaism and heathenism ; and the Jews hated them with a perfect hatred, looking upon them as the worst of all human beings : John viii. 48. At present the Samaritans, though few in number, pretend to observe the law of Moses ; and find great fault with the Jews for their negligence. They circumcise their children on the eighth day after their birth ; and do not allow a plurality of wives; nor marry their nieces. They observe the Sabbath so strictly, that they will scarcely move, except to their synagogues.

The Sadducees, who derived their name from *Sadoc*, their founder, were a sort of Deists. They believed that God was the only immaterial being; that there was neither angel nor spirit ; that there was no resurrection of the dead, nor any future state ; and that men were absolute masters of themselves, and need no assistance to enable them to do either good or bad. They rejected all traditions, and adhered to the texts of the sacred books; though it is very evident they did not understand them. They were, in general, men of wealth ; and, without any restraint upon their corrupt passions and appetites, lived at their pleasure. They were jealous opposers of Jesus Christ and his apostles ; and we never read of the conversion of one of them : Math. xxii. 23–34 ; Acts. v. 17.

The Pharisees, or *Separatists*, were so called because they distinguished themselves from others by a strict manner of life, of which they made profession. They were haughty despisers of the common people, and the greater part of the *doctors of the law*, or *scribes*, were of this sect. They substituted human traditions in the room of God word, and were intolerably proud of their religious attainments, supposing they merited the favor of God by their outward observances. They feasted often, made long prayers, gave much alms, and in all things made a great outward show of religion; but were covetous, proud, unjust, superstitious, and hypocritical. See Luke xviii. 9–14. They were very particular in wearing broad *phylacteries* or *frontlets*, which were scrolls of parchment, four in number, and on which they wrote certain words of the law. On the first piece, they wrote Exod. xiii., from verse 2–10; and on the second, from verse 11–21; on the third, Deut. vi., from verse 4–9; and on the fourth, Deut. xi., from verse 13–21. These they put together, covered them with a piece of hard calf-skin, and bound them upon their foreheads, upon their wrists, and upon the hem of their garments, where they wore them during the morning and evening prayers: Math. xxiii. 5. These customs they founded on what you read in Exod. xiii. 9–16, and Numb. xv. 38, 39. And as the prophets never spoke against the omission of this practice, it seems evident they understood *literally* what was *figuratively* spoken. Read Math. xxiii.

The Herodians shaped their religion to suit the time; and though it is not certain what their particular tenets were. it is plain they had a *leaven* of their own, and that they sought to please men more than God, and more especially Herod. See Mark viii. 15, and xii. 13. But we may consider them rather as a *political* party, than a religious sect.

The Stoics were a sect of heathen philosophers, who prided themselves in an affected indifference to pleasure or pain, as though either were only imaginary; and maintained that all things were determined by *Fate*. They held that a wise man ought never to be moved by joy or grief. This sect appears to have been numerous at Athens when the apostle Paul was there: Acts xvii. 8.

The Libertines were free citizens of Rome, who, being Jews or proselytes, had a synagogue at Jerusalem, peculiar to themselves: Acts vi. 9.

The Epicureans were a sect of heathen philosophers, who followed the doctrines of *Epicurus*, the Athenian. They denied that God either made or governs the world, or in any way whatever interferes with his creatures on earth. They denied the existence of angels and the immortality of the soul. They maintained that happiness consisted in pleasure, but *Epicurus* allowed there was no pleasure but in virtue ; and some of his followers held to the same. Their principles were the very opposite of the *Stoics*, and they flourished about 300 years before the Christian era: Acts xvii. 18.

The Galileans appear to have been a very turbulent, *political* party, formed into a *sect* among the Jews, who refused to be in subjection to any other nation ; and who, by degrees, swallowed up most of the other sects. They held much the same sentiments as the Pharisees ; and, in general, they bore no good character for religion : John vii. 52. They considered it beneath the dignity of a Hebrew to pay a tax to heathens. Their first leader was Judas, the Galilean : Acts v. 37. This sect began the war with the Romans, which was never extinguished till the Jewish nation was completely ruined.

The Nicolaitans are expressly named in the New Testament, Rev. ii. 6, 15 ; but who or what they are is not certain. It is said they reckoned adultery and the use of meats offered to idols indifferent things; and imputed all their wickedness to God as the *cause*. Nicholas, one of the first seven deacons, was a man distinguished for holiness and zeal: Acts vi. 5-7. And as nothing is said about his disgracing his profession as a Christian, we cannot think, with some, that he was the founder of this sect. It is not unlikely that they were the very same with, or, at least, a part of, the Gnostics.

Nazarenes. Christ's dwelling at Nazareth gave rise to his being called a Nazarene: Matt. ii. 23. To be called a Nazarene, was to be called a worthless, despicable man, from whom no good was to be expected, John i. 46. This name was put upon Christ by way of reproach and contempt; they called his followers *Nazarenes,* and this stuck to them all as a nickname, Acts xxiv. 5. No name of reproach for religion's sake should seem hard to us, but we should rather rejoice that we are counted worthy to suffer for Christ, who was called a *Nazarene.*

HEBREW OFFICES REFERRED TO IN THE BIBLE.

The Jewish government has been very fitly called a *Theocracy;* that is, a government immediately superintended by God himself. Hence, when they desired a king, it was considered as rejecting the government of God. See 1 Sam. viii. 7 ; Hos. xiii. 10, 11.

The Patriarchs were the principal fathers of mankind, who lived in the early age of the world, and became famous on account of their long lives and descendants. See Gen., chap. v. The name *Patriarch* signifies head of a family: Acts ii. 29 ; vii. 8 ; Heb. vii. 4.

The Prophets were eminent persons, raised up and inspired by God, among the Hebrews, to be the extraordinary ministers of his dispensations: 2 Pet. i. 21. They continued in succession for more than a thousand years, reaching from Moses to Malachi. God's most usual way of making known his will to the prophets was by inspiration; and this consisted in illuminating and dictating to the mind that which he intended they should proclaim. He appeared to Moses and to Job in a cloud: Numb. xi. 25; Job xxxviii. 1. He spoke to Moses in the burning bush, and upon Mount Sinai: Exod. iii. He spoke to Samuel in the night: 1 Sam. iii. 4. He made known his will to Peter in a vision : Acts x. 11, 12.

The High-Priest was the first character in the Jewish government, and the medium of communication with God. He was consecrated to his office in the most solemn manner; and had two kinds of garments, one of which he wore on ordinary occasions, and the other only once a year, when he went into the Most Holy Place alone: Exod. xxviii. and Lev. xvi.; Heb. iv. 6. The priesthood was confined to the family of Aaron: and the first-born of the oldest branch of it was high-priest, if his body was found entirely free from blemish. Read Exod. xxviii. and xxix.; Lev. xvi. and Heb. iii., v., vii., viii., ix. and x.

The Priests, who were also of the family of Aaron, were the ordinary ministers of religion. It was their duty to offer the daily and other sacrifices, under the direction of the high-priest, etc.

The Levites, who were the descendants of *Levi*, but not of the family of Aaron, were a lower order of persons, inferior in office to the *priests*. They applied themselves to the study of the law, and were dispersed through the country as the ordinary teachers, magistrates and judges of the people. They had no sacred apparel; but though the tribe of Levi was but about the fortieth part of the people, forty-eight cities, with their suburbs, were assigned them for their dwelling, and about one-fifth part of the Hebrew income. Read the following chapters: Exod. vi.; xxxii. 15–28; Numb. iii., iv., viii., x. and xviii. They had much more allotted them than they received; for when religion languished they were poorly paid. See Josh xxi. and Neh. xiii. 10.

The Nethinims were servants who had been given up to the service of the tabernacle and temple; and were employed in doing the more laborious duties of hewing wood and drawing water. They were those Canaanites who by their craft had their lives spared. See Josh. ix. and Ezra viii. 20.

Nazarites were persons devoted to the peculiar service of God for a week, a month, a year, or for life. Some of them devoted themselves by a vow to abstain from all intoxicating drinkers;—let their hair grow without cutting or shaving;—not to enter any house that was polluted by a corpse in it; nor to be present at any funeral. Read Numb. vi. 1–21; Acts xviii. 18; xxi. 23–26. It was extremely wicked to offer them strong drink during their vow: Amos ii. 11, 12. Some were expressly claimed by God, as Samson and John the Baptist: Judges xvi. 17; Luke i. 15. *Nazarite* signifies sanctified, or consecrated.

Scribes and Doctors of the Law, in Scripture language, mean the same thing; and no mention is made of them till Judges v. 14. They were employed to be the Judges, interpreters, and preachers of the law to the people; but the latter office they had no divine right unto. They were mostly of the tribe of Levi. See 1 Chron. xxiii. 24; xxiv. 6, and 2 Chron. xxxiv. 13.

The Publicans, though generally Jews, were particularly odious to their brethren, and may be considered as Roman, rather than Hebrew officers, seeing they were employed as tax-gatherers under the Romans.

THE MIRACLES OF CHRIST.

From the New Testament writers it appears evident that but a very small number of the miracles of Christ are recorded. A MIRACLE is an astonishing effect, either superior or contrary to the laws of nature. We must allow that the laws of nature are all *very good*, but to pretend that they are so fixed that no *miracle* can be wrought, would be to bind the ALMIGHTY down to second causes. And not to give credit to *miracles*, because they are contrary to nature and the common observation of mankind, is stupid

2

beyond degree. For if miracles were not contrary to common observation, or could be produced by *natural* causes, there would be no miracles at all. God has done much—but when he works a miracle, he does a *little* more.

The centurion's servant healed, Matt. viii. 5–13.
The tempest stilled, Matt. viii. 23–27.
Two demoniacs of Gadara cured, Matt. viii. 28–34.
A man sick of the palsy cured, Matt. ix. 1–8.
Jairus' daughter raised, Matt. ix. 18–26.
Two blind men restored to sight, Matt. ix. 27–31.
A dumb demoniac cured, Matt. ix. 32–33.
A man with a withered hand cured, Matt. xii. 10–13.
A blind and dumb demoniac cured, Matt. xii. 22–23.
Five thousand fed, Matt. xiv. 15–21.
Christ walks on the sea, Matt. xiv. 22–33.
Canaanitish woman's daughter cured, Matt. xv. 21–28.
Four thousand fed, Matt. xv. 32–39.
A lunatic possessed of a devil cured, Matt. xvii. 14–21.
Procures tribute-money from a fish, Matt. xvii. 24–27.
Two blind men restored to sight, Matt. xx. 30–34.
The fig tree blasted, Matt. xxi. 18–21.
A demoniac cured, Mark i. 23–28.
Peter's mother-in-law healed, Mark i. 29–31.
A leper healed, Mark i. 40–45.
A man both deaf and dumb cured, Mark vii. 31–37.
A blind man restored to sight, Mark viii. 22–26.
Great draught of fishes, Luke v. 1–11.
Widow's son raised from the dead, Luke vii. 11–17.
A woman with an issue healed, Luke viii. 43–48.
A crooked woman cured, Luke xiii. 11–17.
A man cured of the dropsy, Luke xiv. 1–6.
Ten lepers cleansed, Luke xvii. 11–19.
Malchus' ear healed, Luke xxii. 50–51.
Water turned into wine, John ii. 1–11.
A nobleman's son cured, John iv. 46–54.

A cripple at Bethesda cured, John v. 1–9.
A man born blind restored to sight, John ix. 1–12.
Lazarus raised to life, John xi. 1–46.
Surprising draught of fishes, John xxi. 1–14.

The Parables of Christ.

Parables are *figures* used to represent *truths*. Our Lord, in his parables, has taken similitudes from natural things to represent spiritual things. It was anciently common for philosophers to utter their sentiments in parables. And that the prophets made use of parables is very evident from the following passages: Judges ix. 7; 2 Sam. xii. 1; 1 Kings xx. 39; 2 Kings xiv. 9; Isa. v. 1, etc. The mode of instruction by parables was very common in our Saviour's time; and He carried it to the height of excellence and usefulness. In order to understand a parable, observe:

1st. It is not necessary that the representation be strictly true; nor that all the actions spoken of be strictly just; because the design of the *parable* is not to inform concerning *these*, but some important *truth;*

2d. We must carefully gather the *scope* of the parable from what has preceded or immediately follows it;

3d. Several circumstances may be added in a parable for the sake of decorum, that cannot be illustrated in the explication of it; we must, therefore, chiefly attend to the *design* of the parable itself.

We have the following recorded:
The sower, Matt. xiii. 1–23.
The tares among the wheat, Matt. xiii. 24–30.
The grain of mustard seed, Matt. xiii. 31–32.
The leaven in the meal, Matt. xiii. 33.
The hidden treasure, Matt. xiii. 44.
The pearl of great price, Matt. xiii. 45–46.
The net cast into the sea, Matt. xiii. 47–50.

The unmerciful servant, Matt. xviii. 21–35.
The laborers in the vineyard, Matt. xx. 1–16.
The two sons, Matt. xxi. 28–32.
The wicked husbandmen, Matt. xxi. 33–46.
The marriage feast, Matt. xxii. 1–10.
The man without a wedding-garment, Matt. xxii. 11–13.
The ten virgins, Matt. xxv. 1–13.
The talents, Matt. xxv. 14–30.
The sheep and goats, Matt. xxv. 31–46.
The seed growing secretly, Mark iv. 26–29.
The two debtors, Luke vii. 36–50.
The good Samaritan, Luke x. 25–37.
The rich fool, Luke xii. 13–21.
The servants who waited for their Lord, Luke xii. 41–48.
The barren fig tree, Luke xiii. 6–9.
The lost sheep, Luke xv. 3–7.
The lost piece of money, Luke xv. 8–10.
The prodigal son, Luke xv. 11–32.
The unjust steward, Luke xvi. 1–12.
The rich man and Lazarus, Luke xvi. 19–31.
The importunate widow, Luke xviii. 1–8.
The Pharisee and Publican, Luke xviii. 9–14.
The pounds delivered for trading, Luke xix. 11–27.

REMARKABLE DISCOURSES OF CHRIST.

There can be no doubt but an incredible number of volumes must have been written, had all Christ's discourses been recorded. But Infinite Wisdom saw that such a vast number of holy writings would have allowed us no time for reading anything else; nor even meditating upon what we did read or had expounded unto us; hence God has seen fit to leave us no more than we are capable of improving. The following are some of the most *Remarkable Discourses* delivered by our blessed Lord and Saviour:

Sermon upon the Mount, Matt. v., vi., vii.
Ordination charge to the apostles, Matt. x.
Woes against Chorazin, etc., Matt. xi. 20–24.
Discourse on breach of Sabbath, Matt. xii. 1–8.
Refutation of the false charge, Matt. xii. 22–37.
Discourse on internal purity, Matt. xv. 1–20.
Against giving offence, Matt. xviii.
Directions how to obtain heaven, Matt. xix. 16–30.
Discourse on his own sufferings, Matt. xx. 17–19.
Woes against the Pharisees, etc., Matt. xxiii.
Predictions concerning Jerusalem, Matt. xxiv.
Discourse on the way to Gethsemane, Matt. xxvi. 31–36.
Discourse with his disciples, Matt. xxviii. 16–20.
In the synagogue of Nazareth, Luke iv. 16–32.
Woes against the Pharisees, etc., Luke xi. 37–54.
Discourse on humility and prudence, Luke xiv. 7–14.
Conversation with Nicodemus, John iii. 1–21.
With the woman of Samaria, John iv. 1–42.
Discourse concerning the impotent man, John v.
Discourse on the bread of life, John vi.
Discourse at the feast of tabernacles, John vii.
Discourse on occasion of the adulteress, John viii. 1–11.
Discourse concerning the sheep, John x.
Discourse on washing the disciples' feet, John xiii. 7–20.
Discourse of consolation, John xiv. 1–31.
Discourse on loving one another, John xv. 1–27.
Discourse concerning the Holy Ghost, John xvi. 1–33.

APPEARANCES OF CHRIST AFTER THE RESURRECTION.

1. To Mary Magdalene, John xx. 14; Mark xvi. 9.
2. To the other women, Matt. xxviii. 9.
3. To Peter, 1 Cor. xv. 5; Luke xxiv. 34.
4. To two disciples, as they were going to Emmaus, Mark xvi. 12, 13; Luke xxiv. 13–32.

5. The same day at evening to the apostles, in the absence of Thomas, 1 Cor. xv. 5; Mark xvi. 14; Luke xxiv. 36; John xx. 19, 24.

6. To the apostles, when Thomas was present, John xx. 24–29.

7. In Galilee, at the sea of Tiberias, to Peter, Thomas, Nathanael, James and John, and two others, John xxi. 1–14.

8. To the disciples, on a mountain in Galilee, Matt. xxviii. 16.

9. To more than five hundred brethren at once, 1 Cor. xv. 6.

10. To James, one of the apostles, 1 Cor. xv. 7.

11. To all the apostles assembled together, 1 Cor. xv. 7.

12. To the apostles at his ascension, Luke xxiv. 50, 51; Acts i. 9, 10.

13. To Paul, 1 Cor. xv. 8; Acts ix. 3, 4, 5; xxii. 6–10.

MARYS MENTIONED IN THE NEW TESTAMENT.

1. Mary the mother of Jesus, Matt. i. 18; Luke i. 30.
2. Mary the sister of Lazarus, Luke x. 39; John xi. 1.
3. Mary Magdalene, Luke viii. 2; John xx. 1.
4. Mary the wife of Cleophas, John xix. 25.
5. Mary the mother of Mark, Acts xii. 12.
6. Mary of Rome, Romans xvi. 6.

A COMPLETE LIST OF BIBLE PROPER NAMES.

NOTE.—The Scripture Names have been taken afresh from the Common English Version. In placing the accents, and dividing the words into syllables, the authority of Smart and Dr. Smith has been chiefly followed. Where there are two or more accents placed on a word or its re-spelling, the strong accent is marked thus ('), and the weak accent thus (').

Aalar, ă'a-lar.
Aaron, ă'ron.
Aaronites, ă'ron-īts.
Abacuc, ab'a-kuk.
Abaddon, a-bad'don.
Abadias, ab'a-dī''as.
Abagtha, a-bag'thah.
Abana, ab'a-nah.
Abarim, ab'a-rim.
Abba, ab'bah.
Abda, ab'dah.
Abdeel, ab'de-el.
Abdi, ab'dī.
Abdias, ab-dī'as.
Abdiel, ab'de-el.
Abdon, ab'don.
Abednego, a-bed'ne-go.
Abel, ă'bel.
Abel–Beth–Maachah, ă'bel-beth-mă'a-kah.
Abel–ceramim, ă'bel-sē'ra-mim.
Abel–Maim, ă'bel-mă-im.
Abel–Meholah, ă'bel-mĕ'ho-lah.
Abel–Mizraim, ă'bel-mix-rā'im, or mix'rā-im.
Abel–Shittim, ă'bel-shit'tim.
Abez, ă'bez.
Abgarus, ab'gar-us.
Abi, ă'bī.
Abia, } a-bī'ah.
Abiah, }
Abialbon, ă'be-al''bon.
Abiasaph, a-bī'a-saf.
Abiathar, a-bī'a-thar.
Abib, ă-bib.
Abida, } a-bī'dah, or ab'ī-dah.
Abidah, }
Abidan, ab'e-dan.
Abiel, ă'be-el.
Abiezer, ă-be-ē'zer.
Abiezrite, ă-be-ez'rite.
Abigail, ab'e-găl.
Abihail, ab'e-hăl.
Abihu, a-bī'hū.
Abihud, a-bī'hud.

Abijah, ă-bī'jah.
Abijam, ă-bī'jam.
Abila, ab'e-lah.
Abilene, ab-e-lē'ne.
Abimael, a-bim'ă-el.
Abimelech, a-bim'e-lek.
Abinadab, a-bin'a-dab.
Abinoam, a-bin'ō-am.
Abiram, a-bī'ram.
Abiron, a-bī'ron.
Abisei, ab'e-sē''ī.
Abishag, ab'e-shag.
Abishai, ab'e-shă''ī.
Abishalom, a-bish'a-lom.
Abishua, ab-e-shoo'ah.
Abishur, ab'e-shur.
Abisum, ab'e-sum.
Abital, ab'e-tal.
Abitub, ab'e-tub.
Abiud, a-bī'ud.
Abner, ab'ner.
Abraham, ă'bra-ham.
Abram, ă'bram.
Absalom, ab'sa-lom.
Absalon, ab'sa-lon.
Abubus, a-bŭ'bus.
Acatan, ă'ka-tan.
Accad, ak'kad.
Accaron, ak'ka-ron.
Accho, ak'kō.
Aceldama, a-sel'da-mah.
Achaia, a-kī'ă, or a-kā'yah.
Achaicus, a-kă'e-kus.
Achan, ă'kan.
Achar, ă'kar.
Achaz, ă'kaz.
Achbor, ak'bor.
Achiacharus, ă'ke-ak''a-rus.
Achias, a-kī'as.
Achim, ă'kim.
Achior, ă'ke-or.
Achish, ă'kish.
Achitob, a-kī'tob.
Achmetha, ak'me-tha.
Achor, ă'kor.

Achsa, } ak'sah.
Achsah, }
Achshaph, ak'shaf.
Achzib, ak'zib.
Acipha, as'e-fah.
Acitho, as'e-thō.
Acua, ak'ū-ah.
Acub, ā'kub.
Adadah, ad'a-dah.
Adah, ā'dah.
Adaiah, ad-i'ah.
Adalia, ad'a-lī''ah, or a-dal'e-ah.
Adam, ad'am.
Adamah, ad'a-mah.
Adami, ad'a-mī.
Adar, ā'dār.
Adasa, ad'a-sah.
Adbeel, ad'be-el.
Addan, ad'dan.
Addar, ad'dār.
Addi, ad'dī.
Addo, ad'dō.
Addon, ad'don.
Addus, ad'dus.
Ader, ā'der.
Adiel, ā'de-el.
Adin, ā'din.
Adina, ad'e-nah.
Adino, ad'e-nō.
Adinus, ad'e-nus.
Adithaim, ad'e-thā''im.
Adlai, ad-lā'ī.
Admah, ad'mah.
Admatha, ad'mā-tha.
Adna, } ad'nah.
Adnah, }
Adonai, ad'o-nā-ī.
Adonias, ad-o-nī'as.
Adonibezek, a-dō'ni-bē''zek.
Adonijah, ad'o-nī''jah.
Adonikam, ad'o-nī''kam.
Adoniram, ad'o-nī''ram.
Adonizedec, a-dō'ni-zē''dek.
Adora, a-dō'rah.
Adoraim, ad'ō-rā''im.
Adoram, a-dō'ram.
Adrammelech, a-dram'me-lek.
Adramyttium, ad'ra-mit''te-um.
Adria, ā'dre-a.
Adriel, ā'dre-el.
Aduel, ā'dū-el.
Adullam, a-dul'lam.
Adullamite, a-dul'lam-īt.
Adummim, a-dum'mim.
Aedias, ā'ē-dī'as.
Æneas, ē-nē'as.

Ænon, ē'non.
Agaba, ag'a-bah.
Agabus, ag'a-bus.
Agag, ā'gag.
Agagite, ā'gag īt.
Agar, ā'gār.
Agarenes, ag'a-rēnz.
Agee, ā'je-ē.
Aggeus, ag-gē'us.
Aggrippa, a-grip'pah.
Agur, ā'gur.
Ahab, ā'hab.
Aharah, ā'har-ah, or ā-har'ah.
Aharel, a-har'el.
Ahasai, ā'has-ā''ī, or a-has'ā-ī.
Ahasbai, a'has-bā''ī.
Ahasuerus, a-has'ū-ē''rus.
Ahava, ā'ha-vah, or a-hā'vah.
Ahaz, ā'haz.
Ahazai, a-haz'ā-ī.
Ahaziah, ā'ha-zī''ah.
Ahban, àh'ban.
Aher, ā'her.
Ahi, ā'hī.
Ahiah, a-hī'ah.
Ahiam, a-hī'am.
Ahian, a-hī'an.
Ahiezer, ā'hī-ē''zer.
Ahiham, a-hī'ham.
Ahihud, a-hī'hud.
Ahijah, a-hī'jah.
Ahikam, a-hī'kam.
Ahilud, a-hī'lud.
Ahimahaz, a-him'ā-haz.
Ahiman, a-hī'man.
Ahimelech, a-him'e-lek.
Ahimoth, a-hī'moth.
Ahinadab, a-him'a-dab.
Ahinoam, a hin'ō-am.
Ahio, a-hī'ō.
Ahira, a-hī'rah.
Ahiram, a-hī'ram.
Ahiramites, ā-hī'ram-ītz.
Ahisamach, a-his'a-mak.
Ahishahar, a-hish'a-har.
Ahishar, a-hī'shar.
Ahithophel, a-hith'ō-fel.
Ahitub, a-hī'tub.
Ahlab, àh'lab.
Ahlai, ah-lā'ī, or àh'lī.
Ahoah, a-hō'ah.
Ahohite, a-hō'hīt.
Aholah, a-hō'lah.
Aholiab, a-hō'le-ab.
Aholibah, a-hō'le-bah.
Aholibamah, a-hō'le-bā''mah.

Ahumai, à'hŭ-mā''ĭ, or à-hŭ'mā-ĭ.
Ahuzam, a-hū'zam.
Ahuzzath, a-huz'zath.
Ai, ā'ĭ.
Aiah, ā-ĭ'ah.
Aiath, ā-ĭ'ath.
Aija, ā-ĭ'jah.
Aijalon, } aj'a-lon.
Ajalon, }
Aijeleth Shahar, aj'e-leth shā'hàr.
Ain, ā'in.
Airus, ā-ĭ'rus.
Ajah, ā'jah.
Akan, ā'kan.
Akkub, ak'kub.
Akrabbim, a-krab'bim.
Alameth, al'a-meth.
Alamemlech, a-lam'me-lek.
Alamoth, al'a-moth.
Alcimus, al'se-mus.
Alema, al'e-mah.
Alemeth, al-em'eth, or al'em-eth.
Aleph, al'ef.
Alexander, al'egx-an''der.
Aliah, al'e-ah.
Alian, al'e-an.
Alleluia, al'le-loo''yah.
Allom, al'lom.
Allon, al'lon.
Allon-bachuth, al'lon-bak'uth.
Almodad, al'mo-dad.
Almon, al'mon.
Almon-diblathaim, al'mon-dib'-
la-thā''im.
Alnathan, al-nā'than.
Aloth, ā'loth.
Alpha, al'fah.
Alphæus, } al-fē'us.
Alpheus, }
Altaneus, al'ta-nē''us.
Altaschith, al-tas'kith.
Alush, ā'lush.
Alvah, al'vah,
Alvan, al'van.
Amad, ā'mad.
Amadatha, a-mad'a-thah.
Amadathus, a-mad'a-thus.
Amal, ā'mal.
Amalek, am'a-lek.
Amalekite, a-mal'e-kĭt.
Amam, ā'mam.
Aman, ā'man.
Amana, am'a-nah.
Amariah, am'a-rī''ah.
Amarias, am'a-rī''as.
Amasa, am'a-sah, or a-mā'sah.

Amasai, am'a-sā''ĭ, or a-mas'ā-L
Amashai, am'a-shā''ĭ.
Amasiah, am'a-sī''ah.
Amasis, a-mā'sis.
Amatheis, a-mā'thē-is.
Amathis, am'a-this.
Amaziah, am'a-zī''ah.
Amen, à-men'.
Ami, ā'mi.
Aminadab, a-min'a-dab.
Amittai, a-mit'tā-ĭ.
Ammah, am'mah.
Ammi, am'mĭ.
Ammidioi, am-mid'e-oy.
Ammidoi, am'mid-oy.
Ammiel, am'me-el.
Ammihud, am'me-hud, or ammī'-
bud.
Amminadab, am-min'a-dab.
Amminadib, am-min'a-dib, or am'-
me-nā''dab.
Ammishaddai, am'me-shad-dā''ĭ,
or am'me-shad''dĭ.
Ammizabad, am-miz'a-bad.
Ammon, am'mon.
Ammonite, am'mon-ĭt.
Ammonites, am'mon-īts.
Ammonitess, am'mon-ĭt''es.
Amnon, am'non.
Amok, ā'mok.
Amon, ā'mon.
Amorite, am'or-ĭt.
Amorites, am'or-īts.
Amos, ā'mos.
Amoz, ā'mŏz.
Amphipolis, am-fip'ŏ-lis.
Amplias, am'ple-as.
Amram, am'ram.
Amramites, am'ram-īts.
Amraphael, am'ra fel.
Amzi, am'zĭ.
Anab, ā'nab.
Anael, an'ā-el.
Anah, ā'nah.
Anaharath, an'a-hā''rath.
Anaiah, an-ī'ah.
Anak, ā'nak.
Anakim, an'a-kim.
Anamim, an'a-mim.
Anammelech, a-nam'me-lek.
Anan, ā'nan.
Anani, a-nā'nĭ.
Ananiah, an'a-nī''ah.
Ananias, an'a-nī''as.
Ananiel, a-nan'e-el.
Anath, ā'nath.

Anathoth, an'a-thoth.
Anem, ā'nem.
Anen, ā'nen.
Aner, ā'ner.
Anetothite, an-et'ō-thīt.
Antothite, an'tō thīt.
Aniam, an'e-am.
Anim, ā'nim.
Anna, an'nah.
Annaas, an'nā-as.
Annas, an'nas.
Annuus, an'nū-us.
Anos, ā'nos.
Antilibanus, an'te-lib''a-nus.
Antioch, an'te-ok.
Antiochia, an'te-o-kī''ah.
Antiochians, an'te-o-kī''anz, or an'te-ō''ke-anz.
Antiochis, an-tī'ō-kis.
Antiochus, an-tī'ō-kus.
Antipas, an'te-pas.
Antipater, an-tip'a-ter.
Antipatris, an-tip'u-tris.
Antonia, an-tō'ne-ah.
Antothijah, an'to-thī''jah.
Antothite, an'toth-īt.
Anub, ā'nub.
Anus, ā'nus.
Apame, ap'a-mē, or a-pā'mē.
Apelles, a-pel'lēz.
Apharsachites, a-fār'sa-kīts.
Apharsathchites, a-fär'sath-kīts, or af'ar-sath''kīts.
Apharsites, a-fär'sīts.
Aphek, ā'fek.
Aphekah, a-fē'kah, or af'ē-kah.
Apherema, a-fer'e-mah.
Apherra, a-fer'rah.
Aphiah, a-fī'ah.
Aphik, ā'fik.
Aphrah, af'rah.
Aphses, af'sēz.
Apollos, a-pol'los.
Apollon, a-pol'lon.
Apollyon, a-pol'le-on, or a-pol'yon.
Appaim, ap'pā-im, or ap-pā'im.
Apphia, af'fe-ah.
Apphus, af'fus.
Appii–Forum, ap'pe-ī-fō''rum.
Aquila, ak'we-lah.
Ar, är.
Ara, ā'rah.
Arab, ā'rab.
Arabah, ar'a-bah.
Arabatthane, ar'a-bath-thā''ne.
Arabattine, ar'a-bat''te-nē.

Arabia, a-rā'be-ah.
Arabian, a-rā'be-an.
Arabians, a-rā'be-anz.
Arad, ā'rad.
Aradite, ā'rad-īt.
Aradus, ar'a-dus.
Arah, ā'rah.
Aram, ā'ram.
Aramitess, ā'ram-īt'es.
Aram–naharaim, ā'ram-nā'ha-rā''im.
Aram–zobah, a'ram-zō''bah.
Aran, ā'ran.
Ararat, ar'a-rat.
Ararath, ar'a-rath.
Araunah, a-raw'nah.
Arba, } är'bah.
Arbah, }
Arbathite, är'bath-īt.
Arbattis, är-bat'tis.
Arbite, är'bīt.
Arbonai, är'bon-ā''ī.
Archelaus, är'ke-lā''us.
Archevites, är'kev-īts.
Archi, är'kī.
Archite, är'kīt.
Archippus, är-kip'pus.
Ard, ärd.
Ardath, är'dath.
Ardites, ärd'īts.
Ardon, är'don.
Areli, ar'el-ī.
Arelites, ar'el-īts.
Areopagite, ar'ē-op''a-jīt.
Areopagus, ar'ē-op''a-gus.
Ares, ā'rēz.
Aretas, ar'e-tas.
Areus, a-rē'us.
Argob, är'gob.
Aridai, a-rid'ā-ī.
Aridatha, a-rid'-a-thah.
Arieh, ar'e-eh, or a-rī'eh.
Ariel, ā're-el.
Arimathæa, } ar'e-ma-thē''ah.
Arimathea, }
Arioch, ā're-ok.
Arisai, a-ris'ā-ī.
Aristarchus, ar'is-tär''kus.
Aristobulus, ar'is-tō-bū''lus.
Arkite, ärk'īt.
Armageddon, är'ma-ged''don.
Armenia, är-mē'ne-ah.
Armoni, är-mō'nī.
Arna, är'nah.
Arnan, är'nan.
Arnon, är'non.

(27)

Arod, ä'rod.
Arodi, ä'rod-ī, or ar'ō-dī.
Arodites, ä'rod-īts.
Aroer, ar'ō-er.
Aroerite, a-rō'er-īt.
Arom, ä'rom.
Arpad, är'pad.
Arphad, är'fad.
Arphaxad, är-faks'ad.
Arsaces, är-sä'sēz, or är'sa-sēz.
Arsareth, är'sa-reth.
Artaxerxes, är'tag-zerk''zēz.
Artemas, är'te-mas.
Aruboth, är'oo-both.
Arumah, a-roo'mah.
Arvad, är'vad.
Arvadite, är'vad-īt.
Arza, är'zah.
Asa, ä'sah.
Asael, as'ä-el.
Asahel, as'a-hel.
Asahiah, as'ä-hī''ah.
Asaiah, as-ī'ah.
Asana, as'a-nah.
Asaph, ä'saf.
Asarael, a-sä'rä-el.
Asareel, a-sä're-el.
Asarelah, as'a-rē''lah.
Asbazareth, as-baz'a-reth.
Ascalon, as'ka-lon.
Aseas, a-sē'as.
Asebebia, a-seb'e-bī''ah.
Aseuath, as'e-nath.
Aser, ä'ser.
Aserer, ä'ser-er, or a-sē'rer.
Ashan, ä'shan.
Ashbea, ash'bē-ah, or ash-bē'ah.
Ashbel, ash'bel.
Ashbelites, ash'bel-īts.
Ashchenaz, ash'ke-naz.
Ashdod, ash'dod.
Ashdodites, ash'dod-īts.
Ashdothites, ash'doth-īts.
Ashdoth-pisgah, ash'doth-piz''gah
Asher, ä'sher, or ash'er.
Asherites, ash'er-īts.
Ashima, ash'e-mah.
Ashkelon, ash'ke-lon.
Ashkenaz, ash'ke-naz.
Ashnah, ash'nah.
Ashpenaz, ash'pe-naz.
Ashricl, ash're-el.
Ashtaroth, ash'tä-rōth.
Ashterathite, ash-tē'rath-īt.
Ashteroth-Karnaim, ash'te-rōth-kär'nä-im.

Ashtoreth, ash-tō'reth, or ash'to-reth.
Ashur, ash'ur.
Ashurites, ash'ur-īts.
Ashvath, ash'vath.
Asibias, as'e-bī''as.
Asiel, ä'se-el.
Asipha, as'e-fah.
Askelon, as'ke-lon.
Asmodeus, as'mo-dē''us.
Asnah, as'nah.
Asnapper, as-nap'per.
Asom, ä'som.
Aspalathus, as-pal'a-thus.
Aspatha, as'pa-thah, as-pä'thah.
Asphar, as'fär.
Asriel, as're-el.
Asrielites, as're-el-īts.
Assabias, as'sa-bī''as.
Assabimoth, as-sab'e-moth.
Asanias, as'sa-nī''as.
Asshur, ash'ur.
Asshurim, as-shoo'rim, or ash'ū-rim.
Assideans, as'se-dē''anz.
Assir, as'sir.
Assos, as'sos.
Assuerus, as'sū-ē''rus.
Assur, as'sur.
Assyria, as-sir'e-ah.
Assyrian, as-sir'e-an.
Assyrians, as-sir'e-anz.
Astaroth, as'tä-rōth.
Astarte, as-tär'tē.
Astath, as'tath.
Astyages, as-tī'a-jēz.
Asuppim, a-sup'pim.
Asyncritus, a-siu'kre-tus.
Atad, ä'tad.
Atarah, at'a-rah.
Atargatis, a-tär'ga-tis.
Ataroth, at'a-rōth.
Ataroth-adar, at'a-rōth-ä''där.
Ataroth-addar, at'a-rōth-ad''där.
Ater, ä'ter.
Athach, ä'thak.
Athaiah, ath'ä-ī''ah.
Athaliah, ath'a-lī''ah.
Athanasius, ath'a-nä''she-us.
Atharias, ath'a-rī''as.
Athenians, a-thē'ne-anz.
Athenobius, ath'ē-nō''be-us.
Athens, ath'enz.
Athlai, ath'lä-ī.
Atipha, at'e-fah.
Atroth, at'roth.
Attai, at'tä-ī.

Attalia, at'ta-lī"ah.
Attalus, at'ta-lus.
Attharates, at-thar'a-tĕz, or at-thar-ā'tĕz.
Augia, aw'je-ah.
Augustus, aw-gus'tus.
Auranus, aw-rā'nus.
Aurelia, aw-rē'le-ah.
Auteas, aw-tē'as.
Ava, ā'vah.
Avaran, av'a-ran.
Aven, ā'ven.
Avim, ā'vim.
Avims, ā'vims.
Avites, ā'vīts.
Avith, ā'vith.
Azael, az'a-el.
Azaelus, az'ā-ē"lus.
Azal, ā'zal.
Azaliah, az'a-lī"ah.
Azaniah, az'a-nī"ah.
Azaphion, a-zā'fe-on.
Azara, az'a-rah.
Azarael, az-ā'rā-el.
Azareel, az-ā'rē-el.
Azariah, az'a-rī"ah.
Azarias, az'a-rī"as.
Azaz, ā'zaz.
Azaziah, az'a-zī"ah.
Azbazareth, az-baz'a-reth.
Azbuk, az'buk.
Azekah, a-zē'kah, or az'ē-kah.
Azel, ā'zel.
Azem, ā'zem.
Azephurith, az'e-fū"rith.
Azetas, a-zē'tas.
Azgad, az'gad.
Azia, a-zī'ah.
Aziei, a-zī'ē-ī.
Aziel, ā'ze-el.
Aziza, a-zī'zah, or az'ī-zah.
Azmaveth, az'ma-veth, or az-mā'-veth.
Azmon, az'mon.
Aznoth-tabor, az'noth-tā"bor.
Azor, ā'zor.
Azotus, a-zō'tus.
Azriel, az're-el.
Azrikam, az're-kam.
Azabah, az'ū-bah.
Azur, ā'zur.
Azuran, az'ū-ran, or az-ū'ran.
Azzah, az'zah.
Azzan, az'zan.
Azzur, az'zur.

Baal, bā'al.
Baalah, bā'al-ah.
Baalath, bā'al-ath.
Baalath-beer, bā'al-ath-bē"er.
Baal-berith, bā'al-bē"rith.
Baale, bā'a-lē.
Baal-gad, bā'al-gad.
Baal-hamon, bā'al-hā"mon.
Baal-hanan, bā'al-hā"nan.
Baal-hazor, bā'al-hā"zor.
Baal-hermon, bā'al-her"mon.
Baali, bā'al-ī.
Baalim, bā'al-im.
Baalis, bā'a-lis.
Baal-meon, bā'al-mō"on.
Baal-peor, bā'al-pē"or.
Baal-perazim, bā'al-per"a-zim.
Baal-shalisha, bā'al-shal"e-shah, or bā'al-shal-ī"shah.
Baal-tamar, bā'al-tā"mar.
Baal-zebub, bā'al-zē"bub.
Baal-zephon, bā'al-zē"fon.
Baana, } bā'a-nah.
Baanah, }
Baara, bā'a-rah.
Baaseiah, bā'a-sī"ah, or bā'a-sē"-yah.
Baasha, } bā'a-shah.
Baashah, }
Babel, bā'bel.
Babi, bā'bī.
Babylon, bab'e-lon.
Babylonians, bab'e-lo"ne-anz.
Babylonish, bab'e-lō"nish.
Baca, bā'kah.
Bacchides, bak ke-dez.
Bacchurus, bak-kū'rus.
Bacchus, bak"kus.
Bacenor, ba-se'nor.
Backrites, bak'rīts.
Bago, bā'gō.
Bagoas, ba-gō'as.
Bagoi, bag'ō-ī.
Baharumite, ba-hā'rum-īt, o ba'-ha-rū"mīt.
Bahurim, ba-hū'rim.
Bajith, bā'jith.
Bakbakkar, bak-bak'kar.
Bakbuk, bak'buk.
Bakbukiah, bak'buk-ī"ah.
Balaam, bā'lam, or bā'lā-am.
Balac, bā'lak.
Baladan, bal'a-dan.
Balah, bā'lah.
Balak, bā'lak.
Balamo, bal'a-mō.

Balasamus, ba-las'a-mus.
Balnuus, bal-nū'us.
Balthasar, bal-thā'sar, or bal'thā-sar.
Bamah, bā'mah.
Bamoth, bā'moth.
Bamoth-baal, bā''moth-bā'al.
Ban, ban.
Banaias, ban'ā-ī''as.
Bani, bā'nī.
Banid, bā'nid.
Bannaia, ban'nā-ī''ah.
Bannus, ban'uus.
Banuas, ban'ū-as.
Baptist, bap'tist.
Barabbas, ba-rab'bas.
Barachel, bar'a-kel.
Barachiah, bar'a-kī''ah.
Barachias, bar'a-kī''as.
Barak, bā'rak.
Barhumite, bar-hū'mīt.
Bariah, ba-rī'ah.
Barjesus, bàr-jē'zus.
Barjona, bàr-jō'nah.
Barkos, bàr'kos.
Barnabas, bàr'na-bas.
Barodis, ba-rō'dis.
Barsabas, bàr'sa-bas.
Bartacus, bàr'ta-kus.
Bartholomew, bàr-thol'ō-mū.
Bartimæus, } bàr'te-mē''us.
Bartimeus, }
Baruch, bā'ruk.
Barzillai, bàr-zil'lā-ī.
Basaloth, bas'a-loth.
Bascama, bas'ka-mah.
Bashan, bā'shan.
Bashan-havoth-jair, bā'shan-hā'voth-jā'ir.
Bashemath, bash'e-math.
Basmath, bas'math.
Bassa, bas'sah.
Bastai, bas'tā-ī.
Bath-rabbim, bath-rab'bim.
Bathsheba, } bath-shē'bah, or
Bathshebah, } bath'she-bah.
Bath-shua, bath-shoo'ah.
Bath-Zacharias, bath-zak'a-rī''as.
Bavai, bav'ā-ī.
Bazlith, baz'lith.
Bazluth, baz'luth.
Bealiah, bē'a-lī''ah.
Bealoth, bē'a-loth.
Bean, bē'an.
Bebai, beb'ā-ī, or be-bā'ī.
Becher, bē'ker.

Becherites, bē'ker-īts.
Bechorath, be-kō'rath.
Bectileth, bek'te-leth.
Bedad, bē'dad.
Bedaiah, be-dī'ah.
Bedan, bē'dan.
Bedeiah, be-dī'ah.
Beeliada, bē'el-ī''a-dah.
Beelsarus, bē-el'sā-rus.
Beeltethmus, bē'el-teth''mus.
Beelzebub, bē-el'ze-bub.
Beera, } be'e-rah.
Beerah, }
Beer, bē'er.
Beer-elim, bē'er-ē''lim.
Beeri, bē'er-ī.
Beer-lahai-roi, bē'er-lā-hī''roy.
Beeroth, bē'er-oth.
Beerothite, bē-er'oth-īt.
Beersheba, bē-er'she-bah, or bē'er-shē''bah.
Beeshterah, bē-esh'te-rah.
Behemoth, bē'hē-moth.
Bel, bel.
Bela, } bē'lah.
Belah, }
Belaites, bē'lā-īts.
Belemus, bē'le-mus.
Belial, bē'le-al.
Belmaim, bel'ma-īm.
Belmen, bel'men.
Belshazzar, bel-shaz'zar.
Belteshazzar, bel'te-shaz''zar.
Ben, ben.
Benaiah, be-nī'ah, or be-nā'yah.
Ben-ammi, ben-am'mī.
Beneberak, ben-eb'e-rak.
Benejaakan, ben'e-jā''a-kan.
Benhadad, ben-hā'dad.
Benhail, ben-hā'il.
Benhanan, ben-hā'nan.
Beninu, ben'e-nū, or ben-ī'nū.
Benjamin, ben'ja-min.
Benjamite, ben'jam-īt.
Beno, bē'nō, or be-nō'.
Benoni, be-nō'nī.
Benzoheth, ben-zō'heth.
Beon, bē'on.
Beor, bē'or.
Bera, bē'rah.
Berachah, ber'a-kah.
Berachiah, ber'a-kī''ah.
Beraiah, be-rī'ah.
Berea, be-rē'ah.
Berechiah, ber'e-kī''ah.
Bered, bē'red.

Beri, bē'rī.
Beriah, be-rī'ah.
Beriites, be-rī'īts.
Berites, bē'rīts.
Berith, bḗ'rith.
Bernice, ber-nī'sē.
Beroduch–baladan, be-rō'dak-bal"a-dan, or ber'ō-dak-bal"a-dan.
Beroth, bḗ'rōth.
Berothite, bḗ'rōth-īt.
Berothah, bḗ'rō-thah.
Berothai, bḗ'rō-thā"ī.
Berzelus, ber-zḗ'lus.
Besai, bē'sā-ī.
Besodeiah, bes'ō-dī"ah.
Besor, bē'sor.
Bessus, bes'sus.
Betah, bē'tah.
Betane, bet'a-nē.
Beten, bē'tēn.
Beth, beth.
Bethabara, beth-ab'ar-ah.
Bethanath, beth'a-nath.
Bethanoth, beth'a-noth.
Bethany, beth'a-ne.
Betharabah, beth-ar'a-bah.
Betharam, beth-ā'ram.
Betharbel, beth-àr'bel.
Bethaven, beth-ā'ven.
Bethazmaveth, beth-az'ma-veth, or beth'az-mā"veth.
Beth–baal–meon, beth'ba-al-mē"-on.
Bethbarah, beth-bā'rah.
Bethbasi, beth-bā'sī.
Bethbirei, beth-bir'e-ī.
Bethcar, beth'kàr.
Bethdagon, beth-dā'gon.
Bethdiblathaim, beth-dib'la-thā"im.
Bethel, beth'el.
Bethelite, beth'el-īt.
Bethemek, beth-ē'mek.
Bether, bḗ'ther.
Bethesda, be-thez'dah.
Bethezel, be-thē'zel.
Bethgader, beth-gā'der.
Bethgamul, beth-gā'mul, or beth'-ga-mul.
Bethhaccerem, beth-hak'ser-em, or beth'hak-sē"rem.
Bethharan, beth-hā'ran.
Bethhoglah, beth-hog'lah.
Bethhoron, beth-hō'ron.
Bethjeshimoth, beth-jesh'e-moth.
Bethjesimoth, beth-jes'e-moth.

Bethlebaoth, beth-leb'ā-oth.
Bethlehem, beth'le-em.
Bethlehemite, beth'le-em-īt.
Bethlehem–Ephratah, beth'le-em-ef"ra-tah.
Bethlehem–Judah, beth'le-em-joo"dah.
Bethlomon, beth-lō'mon.
Bethmaachah, beth-mā'a-kah.
Bethmarcaboth, beth-màr'ka-both.
Bethmeon, beth-mē'on.
Bethnimrah, beth-nim'rah.
Bethoron, beth-ō'ron, or beth'o-ron.
Bethpalet, beth-pā'let.
Bethpazzez, beth-paz'zez.
Bethpeor, beth-pē'or, beth'pe-or.
Bethphelet, beth-fē'let.
Bethphage, beth'fa-jē, or beth'fāj.
Bethrapha, beth'ra-fah.
Bethrehob, beth'rē-hob.
Bethsaida, beth-sā'dah.
Bethsamos, beth'sa-mos.
Bethshan, beth'shan.
Bethshean, beth'shē-an.
Bethshemesh, beth-shē'mesh, or beth'she-mesh.
Bethshemite, beth'shem-īt.
Bethshittah, beth-shit'tah, or beth'shit-tah.
Bethsura, beth-shoo'rah.
Bethtappuah, beth-tap'pū-ah, or beth'tap-pū"ah.
Bethuel, beth'ū-el.
Bethul, beth'ūl.
Bethulia, beth'ū-lī"ah, or be-thoo'-lī-ah.
Bethzur, beth'zur.
Betolius, be-tō'le-us.
Betomasthem, bet'ō-mas"them.
Betomestham, bet'ō-mes"tham.
Betonim, bet'ō-nim.
Beulah, be-ū'lah.
Bezai, bē'zā-ī.
Bezaleel, bez"a-lē'el.
Bezek, bē'zek.
Bezer, bē'zer.
Bezeth, bē'zeth.
Bichri, bik'rī.
Bidkar, bid'kar.
Bigtha, big'thah.
Bigthan, big'than.
Bigthana, big'tha-nah.
Bigvai, big'vā-ī.
Bikath–avon, bik'ath-ā"von.
Bildad, bil'dad.

l'e-am.	**Cainan,** kī'nan.
'gah.	**Calah,** kā'lah.
ga-ī.	**Calamolalus,** kal'a-mō''lā-lus.
'hah.	**Calchas,** kal'kas.
'han.	**Calcol,** kal'kol.
l'shan.	**Caleb,** kā'leb.
m'hal.	**Caleb-ephratah,** kā'leb-ef''ra-tah.
e-ah.	**Calisthenes,** ka-lis'the-nēz.
i'nŭ-ī.	**Calitas,** kal'e-tas.
'shah.	**Calneh,** kal'nā.
ber'za-vith.	**Calno,** kal'nō.
ish'lam.	**Calphi,** kal'fī.
hī'ah.	**Calvary,** kal'va-re.
th'ron.	**Camon,** kā'mon.
)e-thin'e-ah.	**Cana,** kā'nah.
, biz-joth'jah.	**Canaan,** kā'nan.
'thah.	**Canaanite,** kā'nan-īt.
as'tus.	**Canaanitess,** kā'nan-īt''es.
, bō'a-ner''jēz.	**Canaanitish,** kā'nan-īt''ish.
	Candace, kan'da-sē, or kan-dā'sē.
k'kas.	**Canneh,** kan'nā.
ok'e-roo.	**Capernaum,** ka-per'nā-um.
)'kim.	**Caph,** kaf.
han.	**Caphtor,** kaf'tor.
	Caphtorim, kaf'tō-rim.
rith.	**Caphtorims,** kaf'tō-rimz.
os'kath.	**Caphar,** kā'fàr.
)r.	**Capharsalama,** kā'far-sal''a-ma.
'̓ō-rah.	**Caphenatha,** ka-fen'a-thah.
:ez.	**Caphira,** ka-fī'rah, or kaf'ī-rah.
oz'kath.	**Cappadocia,** kap'pa-dō''she-ah.
z'rah.	**Carabasion,** kar'a-bā''se-on.
-sз'is.	**Carcas,** kàr'kas.
bū-bas'tēz.	**Carchamis,** kàr'ka-mis.
'kī.	**Carchemish,** kàr'ke-mish.
uk-kī'ah.	**Careah,** ka-rē'ah.
	Caria, kā're-ah.
nah.	**Carme,** kàr'mē.
-'nī.	**Carmel,** kàr'mel.
-sī'ris.	**Carmelite,** kàr'mel-īt.
	Carmelitess, kàr'mel-īt''es.
	Carmi, kàr'mī.
'īt.	**Carmites,** kàr'mīts.
	Carnaim, kàr'nā-im, or kar-nā'im.
ıb'bon.	**Carnion,** kàr'ne-on, or kar-nī'on.
)ul.	**Carpus,** kàr'pus.
l'dis.	**Carshena,** kàr-shē'nah, or kàr'shē-
lēz.	nah.
ne, kā'dēz-bàr'nē.	**Casiphia,** ka-sif'e-ah.
ad'me-el.	**Casleu,** kas'loo.
ar.	**Casluhim,** kas'loo-him.
ēz'ā-rē''ah.	**Casphon,** kas'fon.
hilippi, ses'a-re''ah fil-	**Casphor,** kas'for.
	Caspis, kas'pis.
kī'a-fas.	**Castor,** kas'tor.
	Cathna, ka-thū'ah.

Cedron, sĕ'dron, or kĕ'dron.
Ceilan, sī'lan.
Celo-Syria, sĕ'lō-sir''e-ah.
Cenchrea, sen'kre-ah.
Cephas, sĕ'fas.
Cephirah, se-fī'rah.
Ceras, sĕ'ras.
Cesar, sĕ'zar.
Cesar Augustus, se'zar aw-gus'tus.
Cesarea, sĕs'a-rĕ''ah.
Cesarea Philippi, sĕs'a-rĕ''ah fil-ip'pī.
Cetab, sĕ'tab.
Chabris, kă'bris.
Chadias, kă'de-as.
Chalcol, kal'kol.
Chaldea, kal-dĕ'ah.
Chaldean, kal-dĕ'an.
Chaldeans, kal-dĕ'anz.
Chaldees, kal'dĕz.
Chanaan, kă'nan.
Channuneus, kan'nŭ-nĕ''us.
Charaathalar, kar'ā-ath''a-làr.
Characa, kar'a-kah.
Charashim, kar'a-shim.
Charchamis, kàr'ka-mis.
Charchemis, kàr'ke-mis.
Charcus, kàr-kus.
Charea, kă'rĕ-ah.
Charmis, kàr'mis.
Charran, kar'ran.
Chaseba, kas'e-bah.
Chebar, kĕ'bar.
Chedorlaomer, ked'or-lā''ō-mer, or ke-dor'lā-ō''mer.
Chelal, kĕ'lal.
Chelcias, kel'se as, or kel-sī'as.
Chellians, kel'le-anz.
Chelluh, kel'loo.
Chellus, kel'lus.
Chelod, kĕ'lod.
Chelub, kĕ'lub.
Chelubai, kĕ-loo'bā-ī.
Chemarims, kem'a-rimz.
Chemosh, kĕ'mosh.
Chenaanah, ke-nă'a-nah.
Chenani, ken'a-nī.
Chenaniah, ken'a-nī''ah.
Chephar-haammonai, kĕ'far-hā-am'mō-nā''ī.
Chephirah, ke-fī'rah.
Cheran, kĕ'ran.
Chereas, kĕ'rĕ-as.
Cherethims, ker'eth-imz.
Cherethites, ker'eth-īts.
Cherith, kĕ'rith.

Cherub, ker'ub (a city), cher'ub (an angel).
Chesalon, kĕ'sa-lon.
Chesed, kĕ'sed.
Chesil, kĕ'sil.
Chesulloth, ke-sul'loth.
Cheth, keth.
Chettiim, ket'te-im.
Chezib, kĕ'zib.
Chidon, kī'don.
Chileab, kil'e-ab.
Chilion, kil'e-on.
Chilmad, kil'mad.
Chimham, kim'ham.
Chimhan, kim'han.
Chinnereth, kin'ne-reth.
Chinneroth, kin'ne-roth.
Chios, kī'os.
Chisleu, kis'loo.
Chislon, kis'lon.
Chisloth-tabor, kis'loth-tā''bor.
Chittim, kit'tim.
Chiun, kī'un.
Chloe, klō'ĕ.
Choba, kō'bah.
Chobai, kō'bā-ī.
Chorashan, ko-rā'shan.
Chorazin, ko-rā'zin.
Chozeba, ko-zĕ'bah, or kō'ze-bah.
Christ, krīst.
Christian, krist'yan.
Chronicles, kron'e-klz.
Chub, kub.
Chun, kun.
Chushan-rishathaim, koo'shan-rish'a-thā''im.
Chusi, kū'sī.
Chuza, kū'zah.
Cilicia, se-lish'e-ah.
Cinneroth, sin'ne-roth.
Cirama, sir'a-mah, or sir-am-â'.
Cis, sis.
Citims, sit'imz.
Clauda, klaw'dah.
Claudia, klaw'de-ah.
Claudius, klaw'de-us.
Claudius-Cesar, klaw'de-us sĕ'zar.
Claudius-Lysias, klaw'de-us-lish'e-as.
Clement, klem'ent.
Cleopas, klĕ'o-pas.
Cleopatra, klĕ'o-pā''tra.
Cleophas, klĕ'o-fas.
Cnidus, nī'dus.
Cœlo-Syria, sĕ'lō-sir''e-ah.

Colhozeh, kol-hō'zā.
Colius, ko-lī'us, or kŏ'lī-us.
Colosse, ko-los'se.
Colossians, ko-los'se-anz, or ko-losh'e-anz.
Conaniah, kon'ā-nī''ah.
Coniah, ko-nī'ah.
Cononiah, kŏ'nŏ-nī''ah.
Coos, kŏ'os.
Corbe, kor'bē.
Core, kŏ'rē.
Corinth, kor'inth.
Corinthians, ko-rinth'e-anz.
Corinthus, ko-rinth'us.
Cos, kos.
Cosam, kŏ'sam.
Coutha, kow'thah.
Coz, koz.
Cozbi, koz'bī.
Crates, krā'tēz.
Crescens, kres'senz.
Crete, krēt.
Cretes, krēts.
Cretians, krē'she-anz.
Crispus, kris'pus.
Cush, kush, or koosh.
Cushan, kŭ'shan.
Cushan–rishathaim, kŭ'shan-rish'a-thā''im.
Cushi, kŭ'shī.
Cuth, kuth.
Cuthah, kuth'ah.
Cyamon, sī'a-mon.
Cyprians, sip're-anz.
Cyprus, sī'prus.
Cyrene, sī-rē'nē.
Cyrenian, sī-rē'ne-an.
Cyrenians, sī-rē'ne-anz.
Cyrenius, sī-rē'ne-us.
Cyrus, sī'rus.

Dabareh, dab'a-rā.
Dabbasheth, dab'a-sheth, or dab-bash'eth.
Daberath, dab'e-rath.
Dabria, da'bre-ah.
Dacobi, da-kŏ'bī.
Daddeus, dad-dē'us.
Dagon, dā'gon.
Daisan, dī'san.
Dalaiah, dal-ī'ah.
Daleth, dal'eth.
Dalmanutha, dal'ma-nŭ''tha.
Dalmatia, dal-mā'she-ah.
Dalphon, dal'fon.
Damaris, dam'a-ris.

Damascenes, dam'a-sēnz.
Damascus, da-mas'kus.
Dan, dan.
Daniel, dan'e-el, or dan'yel.
Danites, dan'īts.
Danjaan, dan-jā'an.
Dannah, dan'nah.
Daphne, daf'nē.
Dara, dā'rah.
Darda, där'dah.
Darius, da-rī'us.
Darkon, där'kon.
Dathan, dā'than.
Dathema, dath'e-mah.
David, dā'vid.
Debir, dē'bir.
Debora, } deb'o-rah, or de-bō'rah.
Deborah, }
Decapolis, dē-kap'o-lis.
Dedan, dē'dan.
Dedanim, ded'a-nim.
Dehavites, de-hav'īts.
Dekar, dē'kar.
Delaiah, del-ī'ah.
Delilah, del'e-lah.
Delos, dē'los.
Delus, dē'lus.
Demas, dē'mas.
Demetrius, dē-mē'tre-us.
Demophon, dē'mō-fon.
Derbe, der'bē.
Dessau, des'sā-ū.
Deuel, de-ū'el.
Deuteronomy, dū'ter-on''o-me.
Diana, dī-an'ah.
Diblaim, dib'lā-im, or dib-lā'im.
Diblath, dib'lath.
Dibon, dī'bon.
Dibon–Gad, dī'bon-gad.
Dibri, dib'rī.
Didymus, did'e-mus.
Diklah, dik'lah.
Dilean, dil'e-an.
Dimnah, dim'nah.
Dimon, dī'mon.
Dimonah, dī-mō'nah, or dī'mo-nah.
Dinah, dī'nah.
Dinaites, dī'nā-īts.
Dinhabah, din'ha-bah.
Dionysius, dī'o-nish''e-us.
Diotrephes, dī-ot're-fēz.
Dishan, dī'shan.
Dishon, dī'shon.
Dizahab, diz'a-hab.
Docus, dō'kus.
Dodai, dod'ā-ī.

2

Dodanim, dod'a-nim.
Dodavah, dod'a-vah.
Dodo, dō'dō.
Doeg, dō'eg.
Dophkah, dof'kah.
Dor, dor.
Dora, dō'rah.
Dorcas, dor'kas.
Dorymenes, dor-im'e-nēz.
Dositheus, dos-ith'e-us.
Dothaim, dō'thā-im.
Dothan, dō'than.
Drusilla, droo-sil'lah.
Dumah, dū'mah.
Dura, dū'rah.

Eanes, ē'a-nēz.
Ebal, ē'bal.
Ebed, ē'bed.
Ebedmelech, ē'bed-mē''lek.
Ebenezer, eb'en-ē''zer.
Eber, ē'ber.
Ebiasaph, e bī'a-saf.
Ebronah, ē-brō'nah.
Ecanus, ē-kā'nus.
Ecbatana, ek-bat'a-nah.
Ecclesiastes, ek-klē'se-as''tēz.
Ecclesiasticus, ek-klē'se-as''te-kus.
Ed, ed.
Edar, ē'dar.
Eddias, ed'de-as.
Eden, ē'den.
Eder, ē'der.
Edes, ē'dēz.
Edna, ed'nah.
Edom, ē'dom.
Edomite, ē'dom-īt.
Edrei, ed're-ī.
Eglah, eg'lah.
Eglaim, eg'lā-im, or eg-lā'im.
Eglon, eg'lon.
Egypt, ē'jipt.
Egyptian, ē-jip'shan.
Ehi, ē'hī.
Ehud, ē'hud.
Eker, ē'ker.
Ekrebel, ek're-bel.
Ekron, ek'ron.
Ekronites, ek'ron-īts.
Ela, ē'lah.
Eladah, el'a-dah.
Elah, ē'lah.
Elam, ē'lam.
Elamites, ē'lam-īts.
Elasah, el'a-sah.

Elath, ē'lath.
Eloth, ē'loth.
Elbethel, el-beth'el.
Elcia, el'she-ah.
Eldaah, el-dā'ah.
Eldad, el'dad.
Elead, ē'le-ad.
Elealeh, el-ē'a-lā.
Eleasa, el-ē'a-sah.
Eleasah, el-ē'a-sah.
Eleazar, el'ē-ā''zar.
Eleazurus, el'e-a-zū''rus.
El-elohe-Israel, el-el'ō-hē-iz''-rā-el.
Eleph, el'ef.
Eleutherus, el-ū'ther-us.
Elhanan, el-hā'nan.
Eli, ē'lī.
Eliab, ē-lī'ab.
Eliada, } ē-lī'a-dah, or el'ī-a-dah.
Eliadah, }
Eliadun, ē-lī'a dun.
Eliah, ē-lī'ah, or el'ī-ah.
Eliahba, e-lī'a-bah.
Eliakim, ē-lī'a-kim.
Eliali, ē-lī'a-lī.
Eliam, ē-lī'am, or el'ī-am.
Eliaonias, el-e-a-ō'ne-as.
Elias, ē-lī'as.
Eliasaph, ē-lī'a-saf.
Eliashib, ē-lī'a-shib.
Eliasis, ē-lī'a-sis.
Eliathah, ē-lī'a-thah.
Elidad, ē-lī'dad, or el'ī-dad.
Eliel, ē'le-el.
Eli Eli Lama Sabachthani, ē'lī ē'lī lā'ma sā'bak-thā''nī.
Elienai, el'e-ē-nā''ī.
Eliezer, el'e-ē''zer.
Elihœnai, el'e-hō-nā''ī.
Elihoreph, el'e-hō''ref.
Elihu, ē-lī'hū.
Elijah, ē-lī'jah.
Elika, el'e-kah.
Elim, ē'lim.
Elimelech, ē-lim'e-lek.
Eliœnai, el'e-ē-nā''ī.
Eliphal, el'e-fal.
Eliphalat, ē-lif'a-lat, or el'e-fal''at.
Eliphalet, ē-lif'a-let, or el'e-lal''et.
Eliphaz, el'e-faz.
Elipheleh, ē-lif'ē-lā.
Eliphelet, ē-lif'e-let, or el'e-fel''-et.
Elizabeth, ē-liz'a-beth.
Eliseus, ēl'e-sē''us.

Elisha, } ĕ-lī'shah.
Elishah, }
Elishama, e-lish'a-mah.
Elishaphat, ĕ-lish'a-fat.
Elisheba, ĕ-lish'e-bah, or el'e-shĕ" bah.
Elishua, el'ish-ū''ah.
Elisimus, ĕ-lī'se-mus.
Eliu, ē-lī'ū.
Eliud, ē-lī'ud, or el'ī-ud.
Elizaphan, ĕ-liz'a-fan.
Elizur, ē-lī'zur, or el'e-zur.
Elkanah, el'ka-nah.
Elkosh, el'kosh.
Elkoshite, el'kosh-īt.
Ellasar, el'la-sàr.
Elmodam, el-mŏ'dam.
Elnaam, el'nã-am, or el-nã'am.
Elnathan, el'nã-than.
Eloi, ē-lō'ī.
Eloi Eloi Lama Sabachthani,
ē-lō'ī ē-lō'ī lã'ma sã'bak-thã''nī.
Elon, ē'lon.
Elonites, ē'lon-īts.
Elon–Beth–hanan, ē'lon-beth-hã''nan or ē'lon-beth''ha-nan.
Eloth, ē'loth.
Elpaal, el'pã-al, or el-pã'al.
Elpalet, el'pa-let, or el-pa'let.
Elparan, el-pã'ran.
Eltekeh, el'te-kã.
Eltekon, el'te-kon.
Eltolad, el'tō-lad.
Elul, ē'lul, or ē-lol'.
Eluzai, el'ū-zī''ī.
Elymæans, el'e-mē''anz.
Elymas, el'e-mas.
Elzabad, el'zabad.
Elzaphan, el'za-fan.
Emims, ē'mims.
Emmanuel, em-man'ū-el.
Emmaus, em'mã-us, or em-mã'us.
Emmer, em'mer.
Emmor, em'mor.
Enam, ē'nam.
Enan, ē'nan.
Enasibus, ē-nã'se-bus.
Endor, en'dor.
Eneas, ē'ne-as.
Eneglaim, en'eg-lã''im.
Enemessar, en'e-mes'sàr.
Enenius, e-nē'ne-us.
Engannim, en-gan'nim.
Engaddi, en-gad'dī.
Engedi, en'gē-dī, or en-ged'ī.
Enhaddah, en-had'dah.

Enhakkore, en-hak'kō-rē.
Euhazor, en-hã'zor.
Enmishpat, en-mish'pat.
Enoch, e'nok.
Enon, ē'non, for Ænon.
Enos, ē'nos.
Enosh, ē'nosh.
Enrimmon, en-rim'mon.
Enrogel, en-rō'gel.
Enshemesh, en'shē-mesh, or en-shem'ish.
Entappuah, en'tap-pū''ah.
Epaphras, ep'a-tras.
Epaphroditus, e-paf'ro-dī''tus.
Epenetus, } ē-pē'ne-tus.
Epænetus, }
Ephah, ē'fah.
Ephai, ē'fã-ī.
Epher, ē'fer.
Ephes–Dammim, ē'fes-dam''mim.
Ephesians, ef-ē'she-anz.
Ephesus, ef'e-sus.
Ephlal, ef'lal.
Ephphatha, ef'fa-thah.
Ephraim, ē'frã-im.
Ephraimites, ē'frã-im-īts.
Ephrain, ē-frã'in.
Ephratah, ef'ra-tah.
Ephrath, ef'rath.
Ephrathite, ef'rath-īt.
Ephrathites, ef'rath-īts.
Ephron, ef'ron.
Epicureans, ep'e-kū-rē''anz.
Epicurus, ep'e-kū'rus.
Epiphanes, ē-pif'a-nēz.
Er, er.
Eran, ē'ran.
Eranites, ē'ran-īts.
Erastus, ē-rast'us.
Erech, ē'rek.
Eri, ē'rī.
Erites, ē'rīts.
Esaias, ē-zī'as.
Esar–Haddon, ē'sàr-had''don.
Esau, ē'saw.
Esay, ē'sã.
Eschol, es'kol.
Esdraelon, es'dra-ē''lon.
Esdras, es'dras.
Esebon, es'e-bon.
Esebrias, es'e-brī''as.
Esek, ē'sek.
Eshbaal, esh'bã-al.
Eshban, esh'ban.
Eshcol, esh'kol.
Eshean, esh'e-an.

Eshek, ē'shek.
Eshkalouites, esh'ka-lon-īts.
Eshtaol, esh'tā-ol.
Eshtaulites, esh'tawl-īts.
Eshtemoa, esh-tem'ō-ah, or esh-te-mō'ah.
Eshtemoh, esh'te-mō.
Eshton, esh'ton.
Esli, es'lī.
Esora, ē-sō'rah.
Esril, es'ril.
Esrom, es'rom.
Esther, es'ter.
Etam, ē'tam.
Etham, ē'tham.
Ethan, ē'than.
Ethanim, eth'a-nim.
Ethbaal, eth-bā'al.
Ether, ē'ther.
Ethiopia, ē'the-ō''pe-ah.
Ethiopian, ē'the-ō''pe-an.
Ethiopians, ē'the-ō''pe-anz.
Ethma, eth'mah.
Ethnan, eth'nan.
Ethni, eth'nī.
Eubulus, ū-bū'lus.
Euergetes, ū-er'ge-tēz.
Eumenes, ū'men-ēz.
Eunatan, ū'na-tan.
Eunice, ū-nī'sē.
Euodias, ū-ō'de-as.
Euphrates, ū-frā'tēz.
Eupolemus, ū-pol'e-mus.
Euroclydon, ū-rok'le-don.
Eutychus, ū'te-kus.
Eve, ēv.
Evi, ē'vī.
Evil-merodach, ē'vil-mer-ō''dak, or ē'vil-mer''ō-dak.
Exodus, eks'ō-dus.
Ezbai, ez'bā-ī.
Ezbon, ez'bon.
Ezecias, ez'e-sī''as, or ez'e-kī''as.
Ezekias, ez'e-kī''as.
Ezekiel, ē-zē'ke-el.
Ezel, ē'zel.
Ezem, ē'zem.
Ezer, ē'zer.
Ezerias, ez'e-rī''as.
Ezias, ē-zī'as.
Ezion-gaber, ē'ze-on-gā''ber.
Ezion-geber, ē'ze-on-gē''ber.
Eznite, ez'nīt.
Ezra, ez'rah.
Ezrahite, ez'ra-hīt.
Ezri, ez'rī.

Felix, fē'liks.
Festus, fes'tus.
Fortunatus, for'tū-nā''tus.

Gaal, gā'al.
Gaash, gā'ash.
Gaba, gā'bah.
Gabael, gab'ā-el.
Gabatha, gab'a-thah.
Gabbai, gab'bā-ī.
Gabbatha, gab'ba-thah.
Gabdes, gab'dēz.
Gabrias, gā'bre-as.
Gabriel, gā'bre-el.
Gad, gad.
Gadite, gad'īt.
Gadites, gad'īts.
Gadara, gad'ar-ah.
Gadarenes, gad'a-rēnz.
Gaddi, gad'dī.
Gaddiel, gad'de-el.
Gades, gā'dēz.
Gadi, gā'dī.
Gaham, gā'ham.
Gahar, gā'hàr.
Gaius, gā'us, or gī'us.
Galaad, gal'ā-ad.
Galal, gā'lal.
Galatia, ga-lā'she-ah, or ga-lā'sha.
Galatians, ga-lā'she-anz, or ga-lā'shanz.
Galeed, gal'e-ed.
Galenus, ga-lē'nus.
Galgala, gal'ga-lah.
Galilee, gal'e-lē.
Galilean, gal'e-lē''an.
Galileans, gal'e-lē''anz.
Gallim, gal'lim.
Gallio, gal'le-ō.
Gamael, gam'ā-el.
Gamaliel, ga-mā'le-el.
Gammadims, gam'ma-dimz.
Gamul, gā'mul.
Gar, gàr.
Gareb, gā'reb.
Garizim, gàr'e-zim.
Garmite, gàr'mīt.
Gashmu, gash'mū.
Gatam, gā'tam.
Gath, gath.
Gath-hepher, gath-hē'fer.
Gath-rimmon, gath-rim'mon.
Gaza, gā'zah.
Gazathites, gā'zath-īts.
Gazara, gaz'ar-ah.
Gazer, gā'zer.

Gazera, ga-zē'rah.
Gazez, gā'zez.
Gazites, ga'zīts.
Gazzam, gaz'zam.
Geba, gē'bah.
Gebal, gē'bal.
Geber, gē'ber.
Gebim, gē'bim.
Gedaliah, ged'a-lī''ah.
Geddur, ged'dur.
Gedeon, ged'e-on.
Geder, gē'der.
Gederah, ge-dē'rah, or ged'e-rah.
Gederathite, ged'e-rath-īt.
Gederite, ged'er-īt.
Gederoth, ged'er-ōth.
Gederothaim, ged'e-rōth-ā''im.
Gedor, gē'dor, or ge-dor'.
Gehazi, ge-hā'zī.
Gehenna, ge-hen'nah.
Geliloth, gel'e-loth.
Gemalli, ge-mal'lī.
Gemariah, gem'a-rī''ah.
Genesis, jen'e-sis.
Gennesar, gen-nē'sàr.
Gennesaret, gen-nes'ah-ret.
Genneus, gen-nē'us.
Gentile, jen'tīl.
Gentiles, jen'tīlz.
Genubath, gen'ū-bath.
Geon, gē'on.
Gera, gē'rah.
Gerar, gē'ràr.
Gergesenes, ger'ge-sēnz.
Gergesites, ger'ges-īts.
Gerizim, ger'e-zim.
Gerizites, ger'iz-īts.
Gershom, ger'shom.
Gershon, ger'shon.
Gershonite, ger'shon-īt.
Gershonites, ger'shon-īts.
Gerson, ger'son.
Gerzites, ger'zīts.
Gesem, gē'sem.
Gesham, gē'sham.
Geshem, gē'shem.
Geshur, gē'shur.
Geshuri, gesh'ur-ī.
Geshurites, gesh'ur-īts.
Gether, gē'ther.
Gethsemane, geth-sem'a-ne.
Geuel, ge-ū'el.
Gezer, gē'zer.
Gezerites, gez'er-īts.
Gezrites, gez'rīts.
Giah, gī'ah.

Gibbar, gib'bàr.
Gibbethon, gib'be-thon.
Gibea, } gib'e-ah.
Gibeah, }
Gibeath, gib'e-ath.
Gibeathite, gib'e-ath-īt.
Gibeon, gib'e-on.
Gibeonite, gib'e-on-īt.
Gibeonites, gib'e-on-īts.
Giblites, gib'līts.
Giddalti, gid-dal'tī.
Giddel, gid'del.
Gideon, gid'e-on.
Gideoni, gid'e-ō''nī.
Gidom, gī'dom.
Gihon, gī'hon.
Gilalai, gil'a-lā''ī.
Gilboa, gil-bō'ah.
Gilead, gil'e-ad.
Gileadite, gil'e-ad-īt.
Gileadites, gil'e-ad-īts.
Gilgal, gil'gal.
Giloh, gī'loh.
Gilonite, gī'lo-nīt.
Gimel, gim'el.
Gimzo, gim'zō.
Ginath, gī'nath.
Ginnetho, gin'ne-thō.
Ginnethon, gin'ne-thon.
Girgashite, ger'gash-īt.
Girgashites, ger'gash-īts.
Girgasite, ger'gas-īt.
Gispa, gis'pah.
Gittah-hepher, git'tah-hē''fer.
Gittaim, git'ta-im, or git-ta'im.
Gittite, git'tīt.
Gittites, git'tīts.
Gittith, git'tith.
Gizonite, gī'zon-īt.
Gizrites, giz'rīts.
Goath, gō'ath.
Gob, gob.
Gog, gog.
Golan, gō'lan.
Golgotha, gol'gō-thah.
Goliath, go-lī'ath.
Gomer, gō'mer.
Gomorrah, } gō-mor'rah.
Gomorrha, }
Gorgias, gor'ge-as.
Gortyna, gor-tī'nah.
Goshen, gō'shen.
Gotholias, goth'o-lī''as.
Gothoniel, goth-ō'ne-el.
Gozan, gō'zan.
Graba, grā'bah.

Grecia, grē'she-ah.
Grecians, grē'she-anz, or grē'shanz.
Greece, grēs.
Greek, grēk.
Greeks, grēks.
Gudgodah, gud'gō-dah.
Guni, gū'nī.
Gunites, gū'nīts.
Gur, gur.
Gur-baal, gur-bā'al.

Haahashtari, hā'a-hash''tā-rī.
Habaiah, ha-bī'ah.
Habakkuk, hab'ak-kuk.
Habaziniah, hab'a-ze-nī''ah.
Habbacuc, hab'ba-kuk.
Habor, hā'bor.
Hachaliah, hak'a-lī''ah.
Hachilah, hak'e-lah.
Hachmoni, hak'mō-nī.
Hachmonite, hak'mōn-īt.
Hadad, hā'dad.
Hadadezer, had'ad-ē''zer.
Hadad-Rimmon, had'ad-rim''-mon.
Hadar, hā'dar.
Hadarezer, had'ar-ē''zer.
Hadashah, had'a-shah.
Hadassah, ha-das'sah.
Hadattah, ha-dat'tah.
Hadid, hā'did.
Hadlai, had'lā-ī.
Hadoram, ha-dō'ram, or had'ō-ram.
Hadrach, hā'drak.
Hagab, hā'gab.
Hagaba,
Hagabah, } hag'a-bah.
Hagar, hā'gar.
Hagarenes, hā'gar-ēnz.
Hagarites, hā'gar-īts.
Hagerite, hā'ger-īt.
Haggai, hag'gā-ī.
Haggeri, hag'ger-ī.
Haggi, hag'gī.
Haggiah, hag-gī'ah.
Haggites, hag'gīts.
Haggith, hag'gith.
Hagia, hā'ge-ah.
Hai, hā'ī.
Hakkatan, hak'ka-tan.
Hakkoz, hak'koz.
Hakupha, ha-kū'fah.
Halah, hā'lah.
Halak, hā'lak.
Halhul, hal'hul.
Hali, hā'lī.

Halicarnassus, hal'e-kar-nas''-sus.
Hallohesh, ha-lō'hesh.
Halohesh, ha-lō'hesh.
Ham, ham.
Haman, hā'man.
Hamath, hā'math.
Hamathite, hā'math īt.
Hamath-Zobah, hā'math-zō''bah.
Hammath, ham'math.
Hammedatha, ham-med'a-thah, or ham'me-dā''thah.
Hammelech, ham'me-lek, or ham-mel'ek.
Hammoleketh, ham-mol'e-keth, or ham-mo-lek'eth.
Hammon, ham'mon.
Hammothdor, ham'moth-dor.
Hamonah, ha-mō'nah, or ham'o-nah.
Hamongog, hā'mon-gog.
Hamor, hā'mor.
Hamuel, ha-mū'el, or hā'mū-el.
Hamul, hā'mul.
Hamulites, hā'mul-īts.
Hamutal, ha-mū'tal, or ham'ū-tal.
Hanameel, ha-nam'e-el, or han'-am-e-el.
Hanan, hā'nan.
Hananeel, ha-nan'e-el, or han'an-e-el.
Hanani, ha-nā'nī.
Hananiah, han'a-nī''ah.
Hanes, hā'nēz.
Haniel, hā'ne-el.
Hannah, han'nah.
Hannathon, han'na-thon.
Hanniel, han'ne-el.
Hanno, han'nō.
Hanoch, hā'nok.
Hanochites, hā'nok-īts.
Hanun, hā'nun.
Haphraim, hat-rā'im.
Hara, hā'rah.
Haradah, har'a-dah.
Haran, hā'ran.
Hararite, hā'ra-rīt.
Harbona, } har-bō'nah, or hår'-
Harbonah, } bō-nah.
Hareph, hā'ref.
Hareth, hā'reth.
Harhaiah, har-hī'ah.
Harhas, hår'has.
Harhur, hår'hur.
Harim, hā'rim.
Hariph, hā'rif.

Harnepher, här'ne-fer, or har-nef'er.
Harod, hä'rod.
Harodite, hä'rod-īt.
Haroeh, hä'rō-ā, or ha-rō'ā.
Harorite, hä'rō-rīt.
Harosheth, har'ō-sheth, or ha-rō'-sheth.
Harsha, här'shah.
Harum, hä'rum.
Harumaph, har'ū-maf, or ha-roo'-maf.
Haruphite, har'ū-fīt.
Haruz, hä'ruz.
Hasadiah, has'a-dī''ah.
Hasdrubal, has'droo-bal.
Hasenuah, has'e-nū''ah, or ha-sen'ū-ah.
Hashabiah, hash'a-bī''ah.
Hashabnah, hash-ab'nah.
Hashabniah, hash'ab-nī''ah.
Hashbadana, hash-bad'a-nah.
Hashem, hä'shem.
Hashmonah, hash'mo-nah.
Hashub, hä'shub.
Hashubah, hash-ū'bah.
Hashum, hä'shum.
Hashupha, hash'ū-fah.
Hasrah, has'rah.
Hassenaah, has'se-nä''ah.
Hasshub, has'shub.
Hasupha, has'ū-fah.
Hatach, hä'tak.
Hathath, hä'thath.
Hatipha, hat'e-fah.
Hatita, hat'e-tah.
Hattil, hat'til.
Hattush, hat'tush.
Hauran, haw'ran.
Havilah, hav'e-lah.
Havoth-jair, hä'voth-jä''er.
Hazael, haz'ā-el, or hä'zā-el.
Hazaiah, ha-zī'ah.
Hazar-addar, hä'zär-ad''dar.
Hazar-enan, hä'zär-ē''nan.
Hazar-gaddah, häz'är-gad''dah.
Hazar-hatticon, hä'zär-hat''te-kon.
Hazarmaveth, hä'zär-mā''veth.
Hazaroth, hä'za-roth.
Hazar-shual, hä'zär-shoo''al.
Hazar-susah, hä'zär-soo''sah.
Hazar-susim, hä'zär-soo''sim.
Hazazon-tamar, haz'a-zon-tä''-mär.
Hazel-elponi, hä'zel-el-pō''nī.

Hazerim, hä'ze-rim.
Hazeroth, hä'ze-roth.
Hazezon-tamar, haz'e-zon-tä''-mär.
Haziel, hä'ze-el.
Hazo, hä'zō.
Hazor, hä'zor.
Heber, hē'ber.
Heberites, hē'ber-īts.
Hebrew, hē'broo.
Hebrews, hē'brooz.
Hebrewess, hē'broo-es.
Hebron, hē'bron.
Hebronites, hē'bron-īts.
Hegai, heg'ā-ī, or hē-gä'ī.
Hege, hē'gē.
Helah, hē'lah.
Helam, hē'lam.
Helbah, hel'bah.
Helbon, hel'bon.
Helchiah, hel-kī'ah.
Helchias, hel-kī'as.
Heldai, hel-dä'ī.
Heleb, hē'leb.
Heled, hē'led.
Helek, hē'lek.
Helekites, hē'lek-īts.
Helem, hē'lem.
Heleph, hē'lef.
Helez, hē'lēz.
Heli, hē'lī.
Helias, he-lī'as.
Heliodorus, hē'le-o-dō''rus.
Helkai, hel-kä'ī.
Helkath, hel'kath.
Helkath-hazzurim, hel'kath-haz'zu-rim.
Helkias, hel-kī'as.
Helon, hē'lon.
Heman, hē'man.
Hemath, hē'math.
Hemdan, hem'dan.
Hen, hen.
Hena, hē'nah.
Henadad, hen'a-dad.
Henoch, hē'nok.
Hepher, hē'fer.
Hepherites, hē'fer-īts.
Hephzibah, hef'ze-bah.
Hercules, her'kū-lēz.
Heres, hē'rēz.
Heresh, hē'resh.
Hermas, her'mas.
Hermes, her'mēz.
Hermogenes, her-moj'e-nēz.
Hermon, her'mon.

Hermonites, her'mon-īts.
Herod, her'od.
Herodians, he-rō'de-anz.
Herodias, he-rō'de-as.
Herodion, he-rō'de-on.
Herodes, hȧ-rō'dēz.
Hesed, hē'sed.
Heshbon, hesh'bon.
Heshmon, hesh'mon.
Heth, heth.
Hethlon, heth'lon.
Hezeki, hez'e-kī.
Hezekiah, hez'e-kī''ah.
Hezion, hȧz'e-on.
Hezir, hē'zir.
Hezrai, hez'rā-ī, or hez-rā'ī.
Hezro, hez'rō.
Hezron, hez'ron.
Hezronites, hez'ron-īts.
Hiddai, hid'dā-ī, or hid-dā'ī.
Hiddekel, hid'de-kel, or hid-dek'el.
Hiel, hī'el.
Hierapolis, hī'e-rap''o-lis.
Hiereel, hī-er'e-el.
Hieremoth, hī-er'e-moth.
Hierielus, hī er'e-ē''lus.
Hiermas, hī-er'mas.
Hieronymus, hī'er-ōn''e-mus.
Higgaion, hig-gī'on.
Hilen, hī'len.
Hilkiah, hil-kī'ah.
Hillel, hil'lel.
Hinnom, hin'nom.
Hirah, hī'rah.
Hiram, hī'ram.
Hircanus, hir-kā-nus.
Hittite, hit'tīt.
Hittites, hit'tīts.
Hivite, hī'vīt.
Hivites, hī'vīts.
Hizkiah, hiz-kī'ah.
Hizkijah, hiz-kī'jah.
Hobab, hō'bab.
Hobah, hō'bah.
Hod, hod.
Hodaiah, hod i'ah.
Hodaviah, hod'a-vī''ah.
Hodesh, hō'desh.
Hodevah, ho-d i'vah.
Hodiah, ho-dī'ah.
Hodijah, ho-dī'jah.
Hoglah, hog'lah.
Hoham, hō'ham.
Holofernes, hol'o-fer''nēz.
Holon, hō'lon.
Homam, hō'mam.

Hophni, hof'nī.
Hor, hor.
Horam, hō'ram.
Horeb, hō'reb.
Horem, hō'rem.
Hor-hagidgad, hor-hȧ-gid'gad.
Hori, hō'rī.
Horims, hō'rimz.
Horite, hō'rīt.
Horites, hō'rīts.
Hormah, hor'mah.
Horonaim, hor'o-nā''im.
Horonite, hor'on-īt.
Horonites, hor'on-īts.
Hosah, hō'sah.
Hosea, ho-zē'ah.
Hoshaiah, hosh-ī'ah.
Hoshama, hosh'a mah.
Hoshea, ho-shē'ah.
Hotham, hō'tham.
Hothan, hō'than.
Hothir, hō'thir.
Hukkok, huk'kok.
Hukok, hū'kok.
Hul, hul.
Huldah, hul'dah.
Humtah, hum'tah.
Hupham, hū'fam.
Huphamites, hū'fam-īts.
Huppah, hup'pah.
Huppim, hup'pim.
Hur, hur.
Hurai, hū'rā-ī.
Huram, hū'ram.
Huri, hū'rī.
Hushah, hū'shah.
Hushai, hū-shā'ī.
Husham, hū'sham.
Hushathite, hū'shath-īt.
Hushim, hū'shim.
Huz, huz.
Huzzab, huz'zab.
Hydaspes, he-das'pēz.
Hymenæus, hī'me-nē''us.

Ibhar, ib'hȧr.
Iblaim, ib'lā-im.
Ibleam, ib'le-am.
Ibneiah, ib-nī'ah.
Ibnijah, ib-nī'jah.
Ibri, ib'rī.
Ibzan, ib'zan.
Ichabod, ik'a-bod.
Iconium, ī-kō'ne-um.
Idalah, id'ȧ-lah.
Idbash, īd'bash.

Iddo, Id'dŏ.
Iduel, id'ū-el.
Idumea, id'ū-mē''ah.
Idumeans, id'ū-mē''anz.
Igal, ī'gal.
Igdaliah, ig'da-lī''ah.
Igeal, ig'e-al.
Iim, ī'im.
Ije-abarim, ī'jĕ-ab''a-rim.
Ijon, ī'jon.
Ikkesh, ik'kesh.
Ilai, ī'lā-ī.
Illyricum, il-lir'e-kum.
Imla, } im'lah.
Imlah, }
Immanuel, im-man'ū-el.
Immer, im'mer.
Imna, } im'nah.
Imnah, }
Imrah, im'rah.
Imri, im'rī.
India, in'de-ah.
Iphedeiah, if'e-dī''ah.
Ir, er.
Ira, ī'rah.
Irad, ī'rad.
Iram, ī'ram.
Iri, ī'rī.
Irijah, e-rī'jah.
Irnahash, ir'nä-hash.
Iron, ī'ron.
Irpeel, ir'pē-el.
Irshemesh, ir-shem'esh.
Iru, ī'roo.
Isaac, ī'zak.
Isaiah, ī-zī'ah, or ī-zī'yah.
Iscah, is'kah.
Iscariot, is-kar'e-ot.
Isdael, is'dā-el.
Ishbah, ish'bah.
Ishbak, ish'bak.
Ishbi-benob, ish'be-bē''nob.
Ishbosheth, ish-bō'sheth.
Ishi, ish'ī.
Ishiah, ish ī'ah.
Ishijah, ish-ī'jah.
Ishma, ish'mah.
Ishmael, ish'mā-el.
Ishmaelite, ish'mā-el-īt.
Ishmaelites, ish'mā-el-īts.
Ishmaiah, ish-mī'ah.
Ishmeelite, ish'mē-el-īt.
Ishmeelites, ish'mē-el-īts.
Ishmerai, ish'me-rā''ī.
Ishod, ish'od.
Ishpan, ish'pan.

Ishtob, ish'tob.
Ishua, ish'ū-ah.
Ishuai, ish'ū-a''ī.
Ishui, ish'ū-ī.
Ismachiah, is'ma-kī''ah.
Ismael, is'mā-el.
Ismaiah, is-mī'ah.
Ispah, is'pah.
Israel, iz'rā-el.
Israelite, iz'rā-el-īt.
Israelites, iz'rā-el-īts.
Issachar, is'sa-kär.
Isshiah, is-shī'ah.
Istalcurus, is'tal-kū''rus.
Isuah, is'ū-ah.
Isui, is'ū-ī.
Italian, i-tal'yan.
Italy, it'a-le.
Ithai, ith'ā-ī, or ith-ā'ī.
Ithamar, ith'a-mär.
Ithiel, ith'e-el.
Ithmah, ith'mah.
Ithnan, ith'nan.
Ithra, ith'rah.
Ithran, ith'ran.
Ithream, ith're-am.
Ithrite, ith'rīt.
Ithrites, ith'rīts.
Ittah-Kazin, it'tah-kā''zin.
Ittai, it'tā-ī.
Iturea, it'ū-rē''ah.
Ivah, ī'vah.
Izehar, iz'e-här.
Izeharites, iz'e-här-īts.
Izhar, iz'här.
Izharites, iz'här-īts.
Izrahiah, iz'ra-hī''ah.
Izrahite, iz'ra-hīt.
Izri, iz'rī.

Jaakan, jā'a-kan.
Jaakobah, jā-ak'ō-bah, or jā-kō'-
  bah.
Jaala, } jā'a-lah.
Jaalah, }
Jaalam, jā'a-lam.
Jaanai, jā'a-nā''ī.
Jaare-oregim, jā'ar-ĕ-or''e-jim.
Jaasau, jā'a-sä''ū.
Jaasiel, ja-ā'se-el.
Jaazaniah, jā-az'ā-nī''ah.
Jaazer, jā'a-zer.
Jaaziah, jā'a-zī''ah.
Jaaziel, ja-ā'ze-el.
Jabal, jā'bal.
Jabbok, jab'bok.

Jabesh, jā'besh.
Jabesh-gilead, jā'besh-gil''e-ad.
Jabez, jā'bĕz.
Jabin, jā'bin.
Jabneel, jab'ne el.
Jabneh, jab'nā.
Jachan, jā'kan.
Jachin, ja'kin.
Jachinites, jā'kin-īts.
Jacob, jā'kob.
Jacubus, ja-kū'bus.
Jada, jā'dah.
Jadau, ja-dā'ū.
Jaddua, jad-dū'ah.
Jadon, jā'don.
Jael, jā'el.
Jagur, jā'gur.
Jah, jäh.
Jahath, jā'hath.
Jahaz, jā'haz.
Jahaza, } jā-hā'zah.
Jahazah, }
Jahazael, ja-hā'zā-el.
Jahaziah, jā'hā-zī''ah.
Jahaziel, ja-hā'ze-el.
Jahdai, ja-dā'ī.
Jahdiel, jäh'de-el.
Jahdo, jäh'dō.
Jahleel, jäh'le-el.
Jahleelites, jäh'le-el-īts.
Jahmai, ja-mā'ī.
Jahzah, jäh'zah.
Jahzeel, jäh'ze-el.
Jahzeelites, jäh'ze-el-īts.
Jahzerah, jā-zē'rah.
Jahziel, jäh'ze-el.
Jair, jā'ir.
Jairite, jā'ir-īt.
Jairus, jā'ir-us.
Jakan, jā'kan.
Jakeh, jā'kā.
Jakim, jā'kim.
Jakkim, jak'kim.
Jalon, jā'lon.
Jambres, jam'brēz.
Jambri, jam'brī.
James, jāmz.
Jamin, jā'min.
Jaminites, jā'min-īts.
Jamlech, jam'lek.
Jamnia, jam'ne-ah.
Jamnites, jam'nīts.
Janna, jan'nah.
Jannes, jan'nēz.
Janoah, ja-nō'ah.
Janohah, ja-nō'hah.

Janum, jā'num.
Japheth, jā'feth.
Japhia, } ja-fī'ah.
Japhiah, }
Japhlet, jaf'let.
Japhleti, jaf'lē-tī.
Japho, jā'fō.
Jarah, jā'rah.
Jareb, jā'reb.
Jared, jā'red.
Jaresiah, jā're-sī''ah.
Jarha, jär'hah.
Jarib, jā'rib.
Jarimoth, jär'e-moth.
Jarmuth, jär'muth.
Jaroah, ja-rō'ah.
Jasael, jā'sā-el.
Jashen, jā'shen.
Jasher, jā'sher.
Jashobeam, jā-shō'bē-am.
Jashub, jash'ub.
Jashubi-lehem, jash'ū-bī-lē''hem.
Jashubites, jash'ub-īts.
Jasiel, jā'se-el.
Jason, jā'son.
Jasubus, jas-ū'bus.
Jatal, jā'tal.
Jathniel, jath'ne-el.
Jattir, jat'tir.
Javan, jā'van.
Jazar, jā'zär.
Jazer, jā'zer.
Jaziz, jā'ziz.
Jearim, jē'a-rim.
Jeaterai, jē-at'e-rā''ī.
Jeberechiah, jē-ber'e-ki''ah.
Jebus, jē'bus.
Jebusi, jeb'ū-sī.
Jebusite, jeb'ū-sīt.
Jebusites, jeb'ū-sīts.
Jecamiah, jek'a-mī''ah.
Jechonias, } jek'o-nī''as.
Jeconias, }
Jecoliah, jek'o-lī''ah.
Jeconiah, jek'o-nī''ah.
Jedaiah, jed-ī'ah.
Jeddu, jed'dū.
Jedeus, je-dē'us.
Jediael, je-dī'ā-el, or jed'ī-ā-el.
Jedidah, jed'e-dah.
Jedidiah, jed'e-dī''ah.
Jeduthun, jed'ū-thun.
Jeeli, jē'el-ī.
Jeelus, jē'el-us.
Jeezer, je-ē'zer.
Jeezerites, je-ē'zer-īts.

Jegar-Sahadutha, jĕ'gàr-să'ha-
J dŭ"thah.
Jehaleleel, je-hal'e-lĕ-el.
Jehalelel, je-hal'e-lel.
Jehaziel, je-hā'ze-el.
Jehdeiah, je-dī'ah.
Jehezekel, je-hez'e-kel.
Jehiah, je hī'ah.
Jehiel, je-hī'el.
Jehieli, je-hī'e-lī.
Jehizkiah, je'hiz-kī"ah.
Jehoadah, je-hō'ā-dah.
Jehoaddan, je'hō-ad"dan.
Jehoahaz, je-hō'ā-haz.
Jehoash, je-hō'ash.
Jehohanan, je-hō'hā-nan.
Jehoiachin, je-hoy'a-kin.
Jehoiada, je-hoy'a-dah.
Jehoiakim, je-hoy'a-kim.
Jehoiarib, je-hoy'a-rib.
Jehonadab, je-hon'a-dab.
Jehonathan, je-hon'a-than.
Jehoram, je-hō'ram.
Jehoshabeath, je-hosh'a-bĕ''ath.
Jehoshaphat, je-hosh'a-fat.
Jehosheba, je-hosh'e-bah.
Jehoshua, } je-hosh'ū-ah.
Jehoshuah, }
Jehovah, je-hō'vah.
Jehovah-jireh, je-hō'vah-jī"rā.
Jehovah-nissi, je-hō'vah-nis"sī.
Jehovah-shalom, je-hō'vah-shā"-
J lom.
Jehozabad, je-hoz'a-bad.
Jehozadak, je-hoz'a-dak.
Jehu, jĕ'hū.
Jehubbah, je-hub'bah.
Jehucal, jĕ'hū-kal.
Jehud, jĕ'hud.
Jehudi, je-hū'dī.
Jehudijah, jĕ'hū-dī"jah.
Jehush, jĕ'hush.
Jeiel, jĕ-ī'el.
Jekabzeel, je-kab'ze-el.
Jekameam, jek'a-mĕ"am.
Jekamiah, jek'a-mī"ah.
Jekuthiel, je-kū'the-el.
Jemima, je-mī'mah.
Jemnaan, jem'nā-an.
Jemuel, je-mū'el.
Jephthæ, jef'thē.
Jephthah, jef'thah.
Jephunne, } je-fun'ne.
Jephunneh, }
Jerah, jĕ'rah.
Jerahmeel, je-rā'mĕ-el.

Jerahmeelites, je-rā'mĕ-el-īts.
Jerechus, jer'e-kus.
Jered, jĕ'red.
Jeremai, jer'e-mā"ī.
Jeremiah, jer'e-mī"ah.
Jeremias, jer'e-mī"as.
Jeremoth, jer'e-moth.
Jeremy, jer'e-mī.
Jeriah, je-rī'ah.
Jeribai, jer'e-bā"ī.
Jericho, jer'e-kō.
Jeriel, jer'e-el.
Jerijah, je-rī'jah.
Jerimoth, jer'e-moth.
Jerioth, jer'e-oth.
Jeroboam, jer'o-bō"am.
Jeroham, jer'o-ham.
Jerubbaal, je-rub'bā-al, or je-rub-
bā'al.
Jerubbesheth, jer'ub-besh"eth.
Jeruel, jer'ū-el.
Jerusalem, je-roo'sa-lem.
Jerusha, } jer'ū-shah.
Jerushah, }
Jesaiah, je-sī'ah.
Jeshaiah, jesh-ī'ah.
Jeshanah, jesh'a-nah.
Jesharelah, jesh'a-rĕ"lah.
Jeshebeab, jesh-eb'e-ab.
Jesher, jĕ'sher.
Jeshimon, jesh'e-mon.
Jeshishai, jesh'e-shā"ī.
Jeshohaiah, jesh'o-hī"ah.
Jeshun, } jesh'ū-ah.
Jeshuah, }
Jeshurun, jesh'ū-run.
Jesiah, je-sī'ah.
Jesimiel, je-sim'e-el.
Jesse, jes'se.
Jessue, jes'sū-ē.
Jesu, jēz'ū.
Jesui, jez'ū-ī.
Jesuites, jez'ū-īts.
Jesurun, jes'ū-run.
Jesus, jĕ'zus.
Jether, jeth'er.
Jetheth, jeth'eth.
Jethlah, jeth'lah.
Jethro, jeth'rō.
Jetur, jĕ'tur.
Jeuel, je-ū'el.
Jeush, jĕ'ush.
Jeuz, jĕ'uz.
Jew, joo.
Jewess, joo'es.
Jewish, joo'ish.

Jewry, joo're.
Jews, jooz.
Jezaniah, jez'a-nī''ah.
Jezebel, jez'e-bel.
Jezelus, je-zē'lus.
Jezer, jē'zer.
Jezerites. jē'zer-īts.
Jeziah, jez'e-ah.
Jeziel, jez'e-el.
Jezliah, jez'le-ah.
Jezoar, jez'ō-ȧr, or jez-ō'ȧr.
Jezrahiah, jez'rȧ-hī''ah.
Jezreel, jez'rē-el.
Jezreelite, jez'rē-el-īt.
Jezreelitess, jez'rē-el-īt''es.
Jibsam, jib'sam.
Jidlaph, jid'laf.
Jimna, }
Jimnah, } jim'nah.
Jimnites, jim'nīts.
Jiphtah, jif'tah.
Jiphthahel, jif'thah-el.
Joab, jō'ab.
Joachaz, jō'a-kaz.
Joachim, jō'a-kim.
Joacim, jō'a-sim.
Jondanus, jō'a-dā''nus.
Joah, jō'ah.
Joahaz, jō'a-haz.
Joanan, jō-an'an.
Joanna, jō-an'nah.
Joannan, jō-an'nan.
Joarib, jō'a-rib.
Joash, jō'ash.
Joatham, jō'a-tham.
Joazabdus, jō'az-ab''dus.
Job, jōb.
Jobab, jō'bab.
Jochebed, jok'e-bed, or jok-eb'ed.
Jod, jod.
Joda, jō'dah.
Joed, jō'ed.
Joel, jō'el.
Joelah, jō-ē'lah, or jō'ē-lah.
Joezer, jō-ē'zer.
Jogbehah, jog'be-hah.
Jogli, jog'lī.
Joha, jō'hah.
Johanan, jo-hī'nan, or jō'hȧ-nan.
Johannes, jō-han'nēz.
John, jon.
Joiada, jo-ī'a-dah.
Joiakim, jo-ī'a-kim.
Joiarib, jo-ī'a-rib.
Jokdeam, jok'de-am.
Jokim, jō'kim.

Jokmeam, jok'me-am.
Jokneam, jok'ne-am.
Jokshan, jok'shan.
Joktan, jok'tan.
Joktheel, jok'the-el.
Jonadab, jon'a-dab.
Jona, }
Jonah, } jō'nah.
Jonan, jō'nan.
Jonas, jō'nas.
Jonathan, jon'a-than.
Jonathas, jon'a-thas.
Jonath-elem-rechokim, jō'nath-ē'lem-rē'kō-kim.
Joppa, jop'pah.
Joppe, jop'peh.
Jorah, jō'rah.
Jerai, jo rā'ī.
Jeram, jō'ram.
Jordan, jor'dan.
Joribas, jō're-bas.
Joribus, jō're-bus.
Jorim, jō'rim.
Jorkoam, jor'kō-am.
Josabad, jos'a-bad.
Josaphat, jos'a-fat.
Josaphias, jō-saf'e-as.
Jose, jō'ze.
Josedec, joz'e-dek.
Josedech, joz'e-dek.
Joseph, jō'zef.
Josephus, jō-sē'fus.
Joses, jō'zēz.
Joshah, jō'shah.
Joshaphat, josh'a-fat.
Joshaviah, josh'a-vī''ah, or jo-shav'e-ah.
Joshbekashah. josh-bek'a-shah, or josh'be-kā''shah.
Joshua, josh'ū-ah.
Josiah, jo-sī'ah.
Josias, jo-sī'as.
Josibiah, jos'e-bī''ah, or jo-sib'e-ah.
Josiphiah, jos'e-fī''ah, or jo-sif'e-ah.
Jotbah, jot'bah.
Jotbath, jot'bath.
Jotbathah, jot'ba-thah.
Jotham, jō'tham.
Jozabad, joz'a-bad.
Jozachar, joz'a-kȧr.
Jozadak, joz'a-dak.
Jubal, joo'bal.
Jucal, joo'kal.
Juda, }
Judah, } joo'dah.

Judæa,⎫ joo-dē'ah.
Judea, ⎭
Judas, joo'das.
Judas Iscariot, joo'das is-kar'e-ot.
Jude, jood.
Judges, juj'ez.
Judith, joo'dith.
Juel, joo'el.
Jugurtha, joo-gur'thah, or jug'ur-thah.
Julia, joo'le-ah.
Julius, joo'le-us.
Junia, joo'ne-ah.
Jupiter, joo'pe-ter.
Jushab-hesed, joo'shab-hē''sed.
Justus, jus'tus.
Juttah, jut'tah.

Jabzeel, kab'ze-el.
Jadesh, kā'desh.
Jadesh-Barnea, kā'desh-bär''nĕ-ah.
Jadmiel, kad'me-el.
Jadmonites, kad'mon-īts.
Jallai, kal'lā-ī, or kal-lā'ī.
Janah, kā'nah.
Jareah, ka-rē'ah.
Jarkaa, kär'kā-ah.
Jarkor, kär'kor.
Jaruaim, kär'nā-im, or kar-nā'im.
Jartah, kär'tah.
Jartan, kär'tan.
Jattath, kat'tath.
Jedar, kē'där.
Jedemah, ked'e-mah.
Jedemoth, ked'e-mōth.
Jedesh, kē'desh.
Jehelathah, ke-hel'a-thah, or kĕ'hel-ā''thah.
Jeilah, kī'lah.
Jelaiah, ke-lī'ah.
Jelita, kel'e-tah.
Jemuel, ke-mū'el, or kem'ū-el.
Jenau, kē'nau.
Jenath, kē'nath.
Jenaz, kē'naz.
Jenezite, ken'ez-īt.
Jenite, ken'īt.
Jenites, ken'īts.
Jenizzites, ken'iz-zīts.
Jeren–Happuch,ker'eu-hap''puk.
Jerioth, kē're-oth.
Jeros, kē'ros.
Jeturah, ke-tū'rah.
Jezia, ke-zī'ah.
Jeziz, kō'ziz, or kĕ-ziz'.

Kibroth–hattaavah, kib'roth-hat-tā''a-vah.
Kibzaim, kib'zā-im, or kib-zā'im.
Kidron, kid'ron.
Kinah, kī'uah.
Kings, kingz.
Kir, kir.
Kir–haraseth, kir-har-ā'seth.
Kir–hareseth, kir-har-ē'seth.
Kir–haresh, kir-hā'resh.
Kir–heres, kir-hē'res.
Kiriathaim, kir'e-a-thā''im.
Kiriathiarius, kir'e-ath'e-ā''re-us.
Kirioth, kir'e-oth.
Kirjath, kir'jath.
Kirjath–aim, kir'jath-ā''im.
Kirjath–arba, kir'jath är''bah.
Kirjath–arim, kir'jath-ā''rim.
Kirjath–baal, kir'jath-bā''al.
Kirjath–huzoth, kir'jath-hū''zoth.
Kirjath–jearim, kir'jath-jē''a-rim.
Kirjath–sannah,kir'jath-san''nah.
Kirjath–sepher, kir'jath-sē''fer.
Kish, kish.
Kishi, kish'ī.
Kishion, kish'e-on.
Kishon, kī'shon.
Kison, kī'son.
Kithlish, kith'lish.
Kitron, kit'ron.
Kittim, kit'tim.
Koa, kō'ah.
Kohath, kō'hath.
Kohathites, kō'hath-īts.
Kolaiah, kol-ī'ah.
Korah, kō'rah.
Korahite, kō'rah-īt.
Korahites, kō'rah-īts.
Korathites, kō'rath-īts.
Kore, kō'rē.
Korhites, kor'hīts.
Koz, koz.
Kushaiah, koo-shī'ah.

Laadah, lā'a-dah.
Laadan, lā'a-dan.
Laban, lā'ban.
Labana, lab'a-nah.
Lacedæmon, las'e-dē'mon.
Lacedæmonians, las'e-dē-mō''ne-anz.
Lachish, lā'kish.
Lacunus, la-kū'nus.
Ladan, lā'dan.
Lael, lā'el.
Lahad, lā'had.

Lahairoi, la-hī'roy.
Lahmam, lăh'mam.
Lahmi, lăh'mi.
Laish, lā'ish.
Lakum, lā'kum.
Lamech, lā'mek.
Lamed, lā'med.
Lamentations, lam'en-tā''shunz.
Laodicea, lā-o l'e-sē''ah.
Laodiceans, lā-o l'e-sē''anz.
Lapidoth, lap'e-doth.
Lasea, la-sē'ah.
Lashah, lā'shah.
Lasharon, la-shā'ron, or lash'ā-ron.
Lasthenes, las'then-ēz.
Latiu, lat'iu.
Lazarus, laz'a-rus.
Leah, lē'ah.
Lebana, } leb'a-nah.
Lebanah, }
Lebanon, leb'a-non.
Lebaoth, leb'ā-oth.
Lebbeus, leb-bē'us.
Lebonah, le-bō'nah, or leb'ō nah.
Lecah, lē'kah.
Lehabim, lē'ha-bim.
Lehi, lē'hī.
Lemuel, lem'ū-el.
Leshem, lē'shem.
Lethech, lē'thek.
Lettus, let'tus.
Letushim, let'ū-shim.
Leummim, le-um'mim or lē'um-mim.
Levi, lē'vī.
Levite, lē'vīt.
Levites, lē'vīts.
Leviathan, le-vī'a-than.
Levis, lē'vis.
Levitical, lē-vit'e-kal.
Leviticus, le-vit'e-kus.
Libanus, lib'a-nus.
Libertines, lib'er-tīnz.
Libnah, lib'nah.
Libni, lib'nī.
Libnites, lib'nīts.
Libya, lib'e-ah.
Libyans, lib'e-anz.
Likhi, lik'hī.
Linus, lī'nus.
Loammi, lō-am'mī.
Lod, lod.
Lodebar, lod'e-bär.
Lois, lō'is.
Loruhamah, lō-roo'ha-mah.
Lot, lot.

Lotan, lō'tan.
Lothasubus, lōth'a-sū''bus.
Lozon, loz'on.
Lubim, loo'bim.
Lubims, loo'bimz.
Lucas, loo'kas.
Lucifer, loo'se-fer.
Lucilius, loo-sil'e-us.
Lucius, loo'she-us.
Lud, lud.
Ludim, loo'dim.
Luhith, loo'hith.
Luke, look.
Luz, luz.
Lycaonia, lik'ā-ō''ne-ah.
Lycia, lish'e-ah.
Lydda, lid'dah.
Lydia, lid'e-ah.
Lydians, lid'e-anz.
Lysanias, lī-sā'ne-as.
Lysias, lish'e-as.
Lysimachus, lī-sim'a-kus.
Lystra, lis'trah.

Maacah, mā'a-kah.
Maachah, mā'a-kah.
Maachathi, mā-ak'a-thi.
Maachathite, mā-ak'a thīt.
Maachathites, mā-ak'a-thīts.
Maadai, mā'a-dā'ī.
Maadiah, mā'a-dī''ah.
Maai, ma-ā'ī.
Maaleh-acrabbim, mā'al-ā-a-krab''bim.
Maani, mā'an-ī.
Maarath, mā'a-rath.
Maaseiah, mā'a-sī''ah.
Mansiai, mā'a-sī-ā''ī.
Maasias, mā'a-sī''as.
Maath, mā'ath.
Maaz, mā'az.
Maaziah, mā'a-zī''ah.
Mabdai, mab-dā'ī.
Macalon, mak'a-lon.
Maccabæus, } mak'ka-bē''us.
Maccabeus, }
Maccabees, mak'ka-bēz.
Macedonia, mas'e-dō''ne-ah.
Macedoniau, mas'e-dō''ne-au.
Machbanai, mak'ba-nā''ī.
Machbena, mak'be-nah.
Machi, mā'kī.
Machir, mā'kir.
Machirites, mā'kir-īts.
Machmas, mak'mas.
Machnadebai, mak'na-de-bā''ī.

Machpelah, mak-pē'lah, or mak'-pē-lah.
Macron, mak'ron.
Madai, mā-dā'ī.
Madiabun, mad'e-a-bun.
Madian, mā'de-an.
Madmannah, mad'man-nah.
Madmen, mad'men.
Madmenah, mad'mē-nah.
Madon, mā'don.
Mœlus, mē'lus.
Magbish, mag'bish.
Magdalene, mag'da-lē''nē.
Magdiel, mag'de-el.
Maged, mā'ged.
Magiddo, ma-gid'dō.
Magog, mā'gog.
Magor-missabib, mā'gor-mis''sa-bib.
Magpiash, mag'pe-ash.
Mahalah, mā'ha-lah.
Mahalaleel, ma-hā'la-lē-el.
Mahalath, mā'ha-lath.
Mahalath-leannoth, mā'ha-lath-le-an''noth.
Mahali, mā'ha-lī.
Mahanaim, mā'ha-nā''im.
Mahaneh-dan, mā'ha-ni-dan.
Maharai, mā'ha-rā''ī.
Mahath, mā'hath.
Mahavite, mā'ha-vīt.
Mahazioth, ma-hā'ze-oth.
Maher-shalal-hashbaz, mā'her-shal'al-hash''baz.
Mahlah, māh'lah.
Mahli, māh'lī.
Mahlites, māh'līts.
Mahlon, māh'lon.
Mahol, mā'hol.
Maianeas, mī-an'c-as.
Makaz, mā'kaz.
Maked, mā'ked.
Makheloth, mak-hē'loth, or mak'-hē-loth.
Makkedah, mak-kē'dah.
Maktesh, mak'tesh.
Malachi, mal'a-kī.
Malachy, mal'a-kī.
Malcham, mal'kam.
Malchiah, mal-kī'ah.
Malchiel, mal'ke-el.
Malchielites, mal'ke-el-īts.
Malchijah, mal-kī'jah.
Malchiram, mal-kī'ram.
Malchishua, } mal'ke-shoo''ah.
Malchishuah, }

Malchus, mal'kus.
Maleleel, mal'e-lē-el.
Mallos, mal'los.
Malothi, mal-lō'thī.
Malluch, mal'luk.
Mamaias, ma-mī'as.
Mamnitanaimus, mam'ne-tan-ī''-mus.
Mamre, mam're.
Mamuchus, mam-ū'kus.
Manaen, man'ā-en.
Manahath, man'a-hath, or man-ā'-hath.
Manahethites, ma-nā'heth-īts.
Manasseas, man-as'se-as.
Manasseh, ma-nas'sā.
Manasses, ma-nas'sēz.
Manassites, ma-nas'sīts.
Manetho, man-eth'ō.
Mani, mā'nī.
Manlius, man'le-us.
Manoah, ma-nō'ah.
Maoch, mā'ok.
Maon, mā'on.
Maonites, mā'on-īts.
Mara, } mā'rah.
Marah, }
Maralah, mar'a-lah.
Maranatha, mar'a-nath''ah, or mar'a-nā''thah.
Marcus, mär'kus.
Mardocheus, mär'dō-kē''us.
Mareshah, ma-rē'shah, or mar'ē-shah.
Marimoth, mar'e-moth.
Marisa, mā're-sah.
Mark, märk.
Marmoth, mär'moth.
Maroth, mā'roth.
Marsena, mär'sē-nah.
Martha, mär'thah.
Mary, mā're.
Mary Magdalene, mā're mag'da-lē''ne.
Masaloth, mas'a-loth.
Maschil, mas'kil.
Mash, mash.
Mashal, mā'shal, or mash'al.
Masias, ma-sī'as.
Masinissa, mas'e-nis''sah.
Masman, mas'man.
Maspha, mas'fah.
Masrekah, mas're-kah.
Massa, } mas'sah.
Massah, }
Massias, mas-sī'as.

Mathanias, math′a-nī″as.
Mathusala, ma-thoo′sa-lah.
Matred, mā′tred, or mat′red.
Matri, mā′tri, or mat′rī.
Mattan, mat′tan.
Mattanah, mat′tan-ah.
Mattaniah, mat′tan-ī″ah.
Mattatha, } mat′ta-thah.
Mattathah, }
Mattathias, mat′ta-thī″as.
Mattenai, mat′te-nā″ī.
Matthan, mat′than.
Matthanias, mat′than-ī″as.
Matthat, mat′that.
Matthelas, math-ē′las.
Matthew, math′thū.
Matthias, math-thī′as.
Mattithiah, mat′te-thī″ah.
Mazitias, maz′e-tī″as.
Mazzaroth, maz′za-roth.
Meah, mē′ah.
Meani, mē′a-nī.
Mearah, mē′a-rah.
Mebunnai, mē′bun-nā″ī.
Mecherathite, mek′e-rath-īt, or me-kē′rath-īt.
Medaba, mē′da-bah.
Medad, mē′dad.
Medan, mē′dan.
Mede, mēd.
Medes, mēdz.
Medeba, med′e-bah.
Media, mē′de-ah.
Median, mē′de-an.
Meeda, mē′e-dah.
Megabazus, meg′a-bā″zus.
Megabyzus, meg′a-bī″zus.
Megiddo, me-gid′dō.
Megiddon, me-gid′don.
Mehetabeel, me-het′a-bēl.
Mehetabel, me-het′a-bel.
Mehida, me-hī′dah, or mē′hī-dah.
Mehir, mē′hir.
Meholathite, me-hol′ath-īt.
Mehujael, me-hū′jā-el.
Mehuman, me-hū′man, or mē′hū-man.
Mehunim, me-hū′nim.
Mehunims, me-hū′nimz, or mē′hū-nimz.
Mejarkon, me-jär′kon.
Mekonah, mek′ō-nah.
Melatiah, mel′a-tī″ah.
Melchi, mel′kī.
Melchiah, mel-kī′ah.
Melchias, mel-kī′as.

Melchisedec, } mel-kiz′e-dek.
Melchizedek, }
Melchishua, mel′ke-shoo″ah.
Melea, mē′le-ah.
Melech, mē′lek.
Melicu, mel′e-kū.
Melita, mel′e-tah.
Melzar, mel′zär.
Mem, mem.
Memmius Quintus, mem′me-us kwin′tus.
Memphis, mem′fis.
Memucan, me-mū′kan.
Menahem, men′a-hem.
Menan, mē′nan.
Mene, mē′nē.
Menelaus, men′e-lā″us.
Menestheus, me-nes′the-us.
Meonenim, me-on′e-nim.
Meonothai, me-on′ō-thā″ī.
Mephaath, mef′ā-ath, or me-fā′ath.
Mephibosheth, me-fib′ō-sheth, or mef′e-bō″sheth.
Merab, mē′rab.
Meraiah, mē-rī′ah.
Meraioth, me-rī′oth.
Meran, mer′an.
Merari, mer′ar-ī.
Merarites, mer′ar-īts.
Merathaim, mer′a-thā″im.
Mercurius, mer-kū′re-us.
Mered, mē′red.
Meremoth, mer′e-mōth.
Meres, mē′rēz.
Mereshah, mer′e-shah.
Meribah, mer′e-bah.
Meribah-kadesh, mer′e-bah-kā″-desh.
Merib-baal, mer′ib-bā″al.
Merodach, me-rō′dak, or mer′ō-dak.
Merodach-baladan, me-rō′dak-bal″a-dan.
Merom, mē′rom.
Meronothite, me-ron′o-thīt.
Meroz, mē′roz.
Meruth, mē′ruth.
Mesech, mē′sek.
Mesha, mē′shah.
Meshach, mē′shak.
Meshech, mē′shek.
Meshelemiah, me-shel′e-mī″ah.
Meshezabeel, me-shez′a-bē-el.
Meshilemith, me-shil′e-mith.
Meshillemoth, me-shil′le-moth.
Meshobab, me-shō′bab.
Meshullam, me-shul′lam.

Meshullemeth, me-shul'le-meth, or me-shul-lem'eth.
Mesobaite, mes'a-bā-ĭt, or mes-o'-bā-ĭt.
Mesopotamia, mes'ō-pō-tā''me-ah.
Messiah, mes-sī'ah.
Messias, mes-sī'as.
Meterus, me-tē'rus.
Metheg-Ammah, mē'theg-am''-mah.
Methusael, me-thoo'sā-el.
Methuselah, me-thoo'se-lah.
Meunim, me-ū'nim, or mē'ū-nim.
Mezahab, mez'a-hab.
Miamin, mī'a-min.
Mibhar, mib'hàr.
Mibsam, mib'sam.
Mibzar, mib'zàr.
Micah, mī'kah.
Micaiah, mī-kī'ah.
Micha, mī'kah.
Michael, mī'kal.
Michah, mī'kah.
Michaiah, mī-kī'ah.
Michal, mī'kal.
Micheas, mī-kē'as.
Michmas, mik'mas.
Michmash, mik'mash.
Michmethah, mik'me-thah.
Michri, mik'rī.
Michtam, mik'tam.
Middin, mid'din.
Midian, mid'e-an.
Midianite, mid'e-an-ĭt.
Midianites, mid'e-an-ĭts.
Midianitish, mid'e-an-ĭt''ish.
Migdalel, mig'dal-el.
Migdal-gad, mig'dal-gad.
Migdol, mig'dol.
Migron, mig'ron.
Mijamin, mī'ja-min.
Mikloth, mik'loth.
Mikneiah, mik-nī'ah.
Milalai, mil'a-lā''ī.
Milcah, mil'kah.
Milcom, mil'kom.
Miletum, mī-lē'tum.
Miletus, mī-lē'tus.
Millo, mil'lō.
Milo, mī'lō.
Miniamia, min'e-a-min.
Minni, min'nī.
Minnith, min'nith.
Miphkad, mif'kad.
Miriam, mir'e-am.
Mirma, mir'mah.

Misael, mis'a-el.
Misgab, mis'gab.
Mishael, mish'ā-el.
Mishal, mī'shal.
Misham, mī'sham.
Misheal, mī'she-al.
Mishma, mish'mah.
Mishmannah, mish-man'nah.
Mishraites, mish'rā-its.
Mispar, miz'pàr.
Mispereth, mis'pe-reth, or mis-per'-eth.
Misrephoth-maim, mis're-foth-mā''im.
Mithcah, mith'kah.
Mithnite, mith'nĭt.
Mithredath, mith're-dath.
Mithridates, mith're-dā''tēz.
Mitylene, mit'e-lē''ne.
Mizar, mī'zàr.
Mizpah, miz'pah.
Mizpar, miz'pàr.
Mizpeh, miz'pā.
Mizraim, miz'rā-im.
Mizzah, miz'zah.
Muason, nā'son.
Moab, mō'ab.
Moabite, mō'ab-ĭt.
Moabites, mō'ab-ĭts.
Moabitess, mō'ab-ĭt-es.
Moabitish, mō'ab-ĭt''ish.
Moadiah, mō'a-di''ah.
Modin, mō'din.
Moeth, mō'eth.
Moladah, mol'a-dah.
Molech, mō'lek.
Moli, mō'lī.
Molid, mō'lid.
Moloch, mō'lok.
Momdis, mom'dis.
Moosias, mō'o-sī''as.
Morasthite, mō'ras-thīt.
Mordecai, mor'de-kā''ī, or mor'de-kī.
Moreh, mō'rā.
Moresheth-gath, mor'esh-eth-gath'', or mō-resh'eth-gath''.
Moriah, mo-rī'ah.
Mosera, mō'sē-rah.
Moseroth, mō'sē-roth.
Moses, mō'zez.
Mosollam, mo-sol'lam.
Mosollamon, mo-sol'la-mon.
Moza, } mō'zah.
Mozah, }
Muppim, mup'pim.

4

Mushi, mŭ'shī.
Mushites, mŭ'shīts.
Muthlabben, mŭth-lab'ben.
Myndus, min'dus.
Myra, mī'rah.
Mysia, mish'e-ah, or mī'se-ah.

Naam, nā'am.
Naamah, nā'a-mah.
Naaman, nā'a-man.
Naamathite, nā-am'a-thīt.
Naamathites, nā-am'a-thīts.
Naamites, na'a-mīts.
Naarah, nā'a-rah.
Naarai, nā'a-rā''ī.
Naaran, nā'a-ran.
Naarath, nā'a-rath.
Naashon, nā-ash'on.
Naasson, nā-as'son.
Naathus, nā'a-thus.
Nabal, nā'bal.
Nabarias, nā'bar-ī''as.
Nabathites, nā'bath-īts.
Nabonassar, nā'bon-as''sàr.
Naboth, nā'both.
Nabuchodonosor, nab'ū-kod-ō-
nō''sor.
Nachon, nā'kon.
Nachor, nā'kor.
Nadab, nā'dab.
Nadabatha, na-dab'a-thah.
Nagge, nag'gē.
Nahalal, nā'ha-lal.
Nahaliel, na-hā'le-el.
Nahallal, nā'hal-lal.
Nahalol, nā'ha-lol.
Naham, nā'ham.
Nahamani, na-ham'a-nī, or nā'ha-
mā''nī.
Naharai, nā'ha-rā''ī.
Nahari, nā'har-ī.
Nahash, nā'hash.
Nahath, nā'hath.
Nahbi, nāh'bī.
Nahor, nā'hor.
Nahshon, nāh'shon.
Nahum, nā'hum.
Nain, nā'in.
Naioth, nī'ōth.
Nanea, na-nē'ah.
Naomi, nā'o-mī, or nā-ō'mī.
Naphish, nā'fish.
Naphisi, naf'e-sī.
Naphtali, naf'ta-lī.
Naphthali, naf'tha-lī.
Naphthar, naf'thàr.

Naphtuhim, naf'tū-him.
Narcissus, nàr-sis'sus.
Nasbas, nas'bas.
Naser, nā'ser.
Nasith, nā'sith.
Nathan, nā'than.
Nathanael, na-than'a-el.
Nathanias, nā'than-ī''as.
Nathan-melech, nā'than-mē''lek.
Naum, nā'um.
Nazarene, naz'a-rēn.
Nazarenes, naz'a-renz.
Nazareth, naz'a-reth.
Nazarite, naz'a-rīt.
Nazarites, naz'a-rīts.
Neah, nē'ah.
Neapolis, nē-ap'o-lis.
Neariah, nē'a-rī''ah.
Nebai, neb'ā-ī, or ne-bā'ī.
Nobaioth, ne-bī'oth.
Nebajoth, ne-bā'joth.
Neballat, ne-bal'lat.
Nebat, nē'bat.
Nebo, nē'bō.
Nebuchadnezzar,   neb'ū-kad-
nez''zàr.
Nebuchadrezzar, neb'ū-kad-rēz''-
zàr.
Nebushasban, neb'ū-shas''ban.
Nebuzaradan, neb'ū-zàr''a-dan.
Necho, nē'kō.
Necodan, nek'o-dan.
Nedabiah, ned'a-bī''ah.
Neemias, nē'e-mī''as.
Neginah, neg'e-nah.
Neginoth, neg'e-noth.
Nehelamite, ne-hel'a-mīt.
Nehemiah, nē'he-mī''ah.
Nehemias, nē'he-mī''as.
Nehiloth, nē'he-loth.
Nehum, nē'hum.
Nehushta, ne-hush'tah.
Nehushtan, ne-hush'tan.
Neiel, nē'e-el.
Nekeb, nē'keb, or nek'eb.
Nekoda, ne-kō'dah.
Nemuel, nem-ū'el.
Nemuelites, nem-ū'el-īts.
Nepheg, nē'feg.
Nephi, nē'fī.
Nephis, nē'fis.
Nephish, nē'fish.
Nephishesim, ne-fish'e-sim.
Nephthali, nef'tha-lī.
Nephthalim, nef'tha-lim.
Nephtoah, nef'tō-ah, or nef-tō'ah.

Nephusim, ne-fū'sim.
Nepthalim, nep'tha-lim.
Ner, ner.
Nereis, nē-rē'is.
Nereides, nō-rē'e-dez.
Nereus, nēr'ūs.
Nergal, ner'gal.
Nergal-sharezer, ner'gal-sha-re"-zer.
Neri, nē'rī.
Neriah, ne-rī''ah.
Nerias, ne-rī'as.
Nero, nē'rō.
Nethaneel, ne-than'e-el.
Nethaniah, neth'a-nī''ah.
Nethinims, neth'e-nimz.
Netophah, net'ō-fah.
Netophathai, ne-tof'a-thī.
Netophathite, ne-tof'a-thīt.
Netophathites, ne-tof'a-thīts.
Neziah, ne-zī'ah.
Nezib, nē'zib.
Nibhaz, nib'haz.
Nibshan, nib'shan.
Nicanor, nī-kā'nor.
Nicodemus, nik'ō-dē''mus.
Nicolaitans, nik'ō-lā''e-tanz.
Nicolas, nik'ō-las.
Nicopolis, nī-kop'o-lis.
Niger, nī'jer.
Nimrah, nim'rah.
Nimrim, nim'rim.
Nimrod, nim'rod.
Nimshi, nim'shī.
Nineveh, nin'e-vā.
Ninevites, nin'e-vīts.
Nisan, nī'san.
Nison, nī'son.
Nisroch, nis'rok.
No, nō.
Noadiah, nō'a-dī''ah.
Noah, nō'ah.
Nob, nob.
Nobah, nō'bah.
Nod, nod.
Nodab, nō'dab.
Noe, nō'ē.
Noeba, nō-ē'bah.
Nogah, nō'gah.
Nohah, nō'hah.
Non, non.
Noph, nof.
Nophah, nō'fah.
Numbers, num'berz.
Nun, nun.
Nymphas, nim'fas.

Obadiah, ō'ba-dī''ah.
Obal, ō'bal.
Obdia, ob-dī'ah.
Obed, ō'bed.
Obed-edom, ō'bed-ē''dom.
Obeth, ō'beth.
Obil, ō'bil.
Oboth, ō'both.
Ochiel, o-kī'el.
Ocidelus, ō'se-dē''lus.
Ocina, o-sī'nah.
Ocran, ok'ran.
Oded, ō'ded.
Odollam, o-dol'lam.
Odonarkes, od'ō-nàr''kēz.
Og, og.
Ohad, ō'had.
Ohel, ō'hel.
Olamus, ō'lā'mus.
Olives, ol'ivz.
Olivet, ol'e-vet.
Olympas, o-lim'pas.
Olympius, o-lim'pe-us.
Omærus, o-mē'rus.
Omar, ō'màr.
Omega, ō'me-gah.
Omri, om'rī.
On, on.
Onam, ō'nam.
Onan, ō'nan.
Onesimus, on-ēs'e-mus.
Onesiphorus, on'ē-sif'o-rus.
Oniares, on'e-ā''rēz.
Onias, o-nī'as.
Ono, ō'nō.
Ophel, ō'fel.
Ophir, ō'fir.
Ophni, of'nī.
Ophrah, of'rah.
Oreb, ō'reb.
Oren, ō'ren.
Orion, o-rī'on.
Ornan, or'nan.
Orpah, or'pah.
Orthosias, or-thō'se-as.
Osaias, o-sī'as.
Osea, o-sē'ah.
Oseas, o-se'as.
Osee, o'zē.
Oshea, ō'shē-ah.
Othni, oth'nī.
Othniel, oth'ne-el.
Othonias, oth'o-nī''as.
Ozem, ō'zem.
Ozias, o-zī'as.
Oziel, ō'ze-el.

Ozni, oz'ni.
Oznites, oz'nīts.
Ozora, oz-ō'rah.

Paarai, pā'a-rā''ī.
Padan, pā'dan.
Padan-aram, pā'dan-ā''ram.
Padon, pā'don.
Pagiel, pā'ge-el.
Pahath-moab, pā'hath-mō''ab.
Pai, pā'ī.
Palal, pā'lal.
Palestina, pal'es-tī''nah.
Palestine, pal'es-tīn.
Pallu, pal'lū.
Palluites, pal'lū-īts.
Palti, pal'tī.
Paltite, pal'tīt.
Paltiel, pal'te-el.
Pamphylia, pam-fil'e-ah.
Pannag, pan'nag.
Paphos, pā'fos.
Parah, pā'rah.
Paran, pā'ran.
Parbar, pàr'bàr.
Parmashta, pàr-mash'tah.
Parmenas, pàr'me-nas.
Parnach, pàr'nak.
Parosh, pā'rosh.
Parshandatha, pàr-shan'da-thah,
    or pàr-shan-dā'thah.
Parthia, pàr'the-ah.
Parthians, pàr'the-anz.
Paruah, pàr'ū-ah, or par-ū'ah.
Pasach, pā'sak.
Pasdammim, pas-dam'mim.
Paseah, pa-sē'ah.
Pashur, pash'ur.
Patara, pat'a-rah.
Patheus, pa-thē'us.
Pathros, path'ros.
Pathrusim, path'roo-sim.
Patmos, pat'mos.
Patrobas, pat'ro-bas.
Patroclus, pa-trok'lus.
Pau, pā'ū.
Paul, pawl.
Paulus, paw'lus.
Pedahel, ped'a-hel.
Pedahzur, ped'a-zur, or ped-àh'zur.
Pedaiah, ped-ī'ah.
Pekah, pē'kah.
Pekahiah, pek'a-hī''ah.
Pekod, pē'kod.
Pelaiah, pel-ī'ah.
Pelaliah, pel'a-lī''ah.

Pelatiah, pel'a-tī''ah.
Peleg, pē'leg.
Pelet, pē'let.
Peleth, pē'leth.
Pelethites, pē'leth-īts.
Pelias, pe-lī'as.
Pelonite, pel'ō-nīt.
Peniel, pen'e-el.
Peninnah, pe-nin'nah.
Penuel, pe-nū'el, or pen'ū-el.
Peor, pē'or.
Perazim, per'a-zim.
Peresh, pē'resh.
Perez, pē'rēz.
Perez-Uzzah, or **Uzza,** pē'rēz-
    uz''zah.
Perga, per'gah.
Pergamos, per'ga-mos.
Perida, pe-rī'dah, or per'ī-dah.
Perizzite, per'iz-zīt.
Perizzites, per'iz-zīts.
Persepolis, per-sep'o-lis.
Perseus, pers'ūs.
Persia, per'she-ah.
Persians, per'shanz.
Persis, per'sis.
Peruda, per'u-dah, or per-ū'dah.
Peter, pē'tr.
Pethahiah, peth'a-hī''ah.
Pethor, pē'thor.
Pethuel, pe-thū'el, or peth'ū-el.
Peulthai, pē'ul-thā''ī.
Phaath-moab, fā'ath-mō'ab.
Phacareth, fa-kar'eth.
Phaisur, fī'sur.
Phaldaius, fal-dī'us.
Phaleas, fa-lē'as.
Phalec, fā'lek.
Phallu, fal'lū.
Phalti, fal'tī.
Phaltiel, fal'te-el.
Phanuel, fa-nū'el, or fan'ū-el.
Pharacim, far'a-sim.
Pharaoh, fā'rō.
Pharaoh-Hophra, fā'rō-hof'ra.
Pharaoh-necho, } fā'rō-nē''kō.
Pharaoh-nechoh, }
Pharathoni, fā'ra-thō''nī.
Phares, } fā'rēz.
Pharez, }
Pharezites, fā'rēz-īts.
Pharzites, far'zīts.
Pharira, far'e-rah.
Pharisees, far'e-sēz.
Pharosh, fā'rosh.
Pharpar, fàr'pàr.

Phascah, fä'se-ah, or fä-sē'ah.
Phasclis, fa-sē'lis.
Phasirou, fas'e-ron.
Phassaron, fas'sa-ron.
Phebe, fē'bē.
Phenice, fō-nī'sē.
Phenicia, fē-nish'e-ah.
Pheresites, fer'e-sīts.
Pherezites, fer'e-zīts.
Phibeseth, fib'e-seth.
Phichol, fī'kōl.
Philadelphia, fil'a-del"fe-ah.
Philarches, fil-àr'kēz.
Philemon, fī-lē'mon.
Philetus, fī-lē'tus.
Philip, fil'ip.
Philippi, fe-lip'pī.
Philippians, fe-lip'pe-anz.
Philippus, fe-lip'pus.
Philistia, fe-lis'te-ah.
Philistine, fil'is-tin.
Philistines, fil'is-tinz.
Philologus, fe-lol'o-gus.
Phinees, fin'e-es.
Phinehas, fin'e-has.
Phison, fī'son.
Phlegon, fleg'on.
Phoros, fō'ros.
Phrygia, frĭj'e-ah.
Phud, fud.
Phurah, fū'rah.
Phurim, fū'rim.
Phut, fut.
Phuvah, fū'vah.
Phygellus, fe-jel'lus.
Pibeseth, pī-bes'eth.
Pihahiroth, pī'hā-hī"roth.
Pilate, pī'lāt.
Pildash, pil'dash.
Pileha, pil'e-hah.
Piltai, pil'tā-ī.
Pinon, pī'non.
Pira, pī'rah.
Piram, pī'ram.
Pirathon, pir'a-thon.
Pirathonite, pir-ath'on-īt.
Pisgah, piz'gah.
Pisidia, pe-sid'e-ah.
Pison, pī'son.
Pispah, pis'pah.
Pithom, pī'thom.
Pithon, pī'thon.
Pleiades, plī'a-dēz.
Pleiads, plī'adz.
Pochereth, po-ker'eth.
Pontius Pilate, pon'shus pī'lāt.

Pontus, pon'tus.
Poratha, por'a-thah.
Porcius Festus, por'she-us fes'tus.
Posidonius, pos'e-dō"ne-us.
Potiphar, pot'e-fär.
Potipherah, po-tif'er-ah, or pot'if-ē"rah.
Prisca, pris'ka.
Priscilla, pris-sil'lah.
Prochorus, prok'o-rus.
Ptolemais, tol'e-mā"is.
Ptolemce, tol'e-mē"ē.
Ptolemeus, } tol'e-mē"us.
Ptolemæus, }
Pua, } pū'ah.
Puah, }
Publius, pub'le-us.
Pudens, pū'denz.
Puhites, pū'hīts.
Pul, pul.
Punites, pū'nīts.
Punon, pū'non.
Pur, pur.
Purim, pū'rim.
Put, put.
Puteoli, pu-tē'o-lī.
Putiel, pū-te-el.

Quartus, kwàr'tus.
Quintus Memmius, kwin'tus mem'me-us.

Raamah, rā'a-mah.
Raamiah, rā'a-mī"ah.
Raamses, rā-am'sēz.
Rabbah, rab'bah.
Rabbath, rab'bath.
Rabbith, rab'bith.
Rabboni, rab-bō'nī.
Rab-mag, rab'mag.
Rabsaces, rab'sa-sēz.
Rabsares, rab'sa-rēz.
Rabshakeh, rab'sha-kā.
Raca, rā'kah.
Rachab, rā'kab.
Rachal, rā'kal.
Rachel, rā'chel.
Raddai, rad-dā'ī.
Ragau, ra-gā'ū, or rā'gaw.
Rages, rā'gēz.
Raguel, rag'ū-el.
Rahab, rā'hab.
Raham, rā'ham.
Rahel, rā'hel.
Rakem, rā'kem.
Rakkath, rak'kath.

Rakkon, rak'kon.
Ram, ram.
Rama, } rä'mah.
Ramah, }
Ramath, rä'math.
Ramathaim-zophim, rä'math-ā''-im-zō'fim.
Ramathem, rä'math-em.
Ramathite, rä'math-īt.
Ramath-lehi, rä'math-lē''hī.
Ramath-mispeh, rä'math-miz''pā.
Rameses, ra-mē'sēz, or ram'e-sēz.
Ramiah, ra-mī'ah.
Ramoth, rä'moth.
Ramoth-gilead, rä'moth-gil''e-ad.
Rapha, rä'fah.
Raphael, raf'ā-el.
Raphaim, ra-fā'im.
Raphon, rä'fon.
Raphu, rä'fū.
Rasses, ras'sēz.
Rathumus, rath'ū-mus.
Razis, rä'zis.
Reaia, } rē-ī'ah.
Reaiah, }
Reba, rē'bah.
Rebecca, re-bek'kah.
Rebekah, re-bek'ah.
Rechab, rē'kab.
Rechabites, rē'kab-īts, or rek'ab-īts.
Rechah, rē'kah.
Reelaiah, rē'el-ī''ah.
Reelius, re-ē'le-us.
Reesaias, rē'es-ī''as.
Regem, rē'jem.
Regem-melech, rē'jem-mē''lek.
Rehabiah, rē'ha-bī''ah.
Rehob, rē'hob.
Rehoboam, rē'ho-bō''am.
Rehoboth, rē'ho-both.
Rehum, rē'hum.
Rei, rē'ī.
Rekem, rē'kem.
Remaliah, rem'a-lī''ah.
Remeth, rē'meth.
Remmon-methoar, rem'mon-meth''o-àr.
Remphan, rem'fan.
Rephael, ref'a-el.
Rephah, rē'fah.
Rephaiah, ref'ā-ī''ah.
Rephaim, ref'ā-im.
Rephaims, ref'ā-imz.
Rephidim, ref'e-dim.
Resen, rē'sen.

Resheph, rē'shef.
Reu, rē'ū.
Reuben, roo'ben.
Reubenite, roo'ben-īt.
Reubenites, roo'ben-īts.
Reuel, re-ū'el.
Reumah, rē'ū-mah.
Rezeph, rē'zef.
Rezia, re-zī'ah.
Rezin, rē'zin.
Rezon, rē'zon.
Rhegium, rē'je-um.
Rhesa, rē'sah.
Rhoda, rō'dah.
Rhodes, rōdz.
Rhodocus, rod'o-kus.
Rhodus, rō'dus.
Ribai, re-bā'ī.
Riblah, rib'lah.
Rimmon, rim'mon.
Rimmon-parez, rim'mon-pā''rez.
Rinnah, rin'nah.
Riphath, rī'fath.
Rissah, ris'sah.
Rithmah, rith'mah.
Rizpah, riz'pah.
Roboam, ro-bō'am.
Rogelim, rō-gē'lim.
Rohgah, rō'gah.
Roimus, rō'e-mus.
Romamti-ezer, ro-mam'te-ē''zer.
Roman, rō'man.
Romans, rō'manz.
Rome, rōm.
Rosh, rosh.
Rufus, roo'fus.
Ruhamah, roo-hā'mah.
Rumah, roo'mah.
Ruth, rooth.

Sabacthani, sä'bak-thä''nī.
Sabaoth, sa-bā'oth.
Sabat, sä'bat.
Sabateas, sä'ba-tē''as.
Sabatus, sab'a-tus.
Sabban, sab'ban.
Sabbatheus, sab'ba-thē''us.
Sabbeus, sab-bē'us.
Sabeans, sa-bē'anz.
Sabi, sä'bī.
Sabta, } sab'tah.
Sabtah, }
Sabtecha, sab'te-kah.
Sacar, sä'kàr.
Sadamias, sad'a-mī''as.
Sadas, sä'das.

Saddeus, sad-dĕ'us.
Sadduc, sad'duk.
Sadducees, sad'dū-sēz.
Sadoc, sā'dok.
Sala, } sā'lah.
Salah, }
Salamis, sal'a-mis.
Salasadai, sal'a-sad-ā''ī.
Salathiel, sa-lā'the-el.
Salcah, } sal'kah.
Salchah, }
Salem, sā'lem.
Salim, sā'lim.
Sallai, sal-lā'ī.
Sallu, sal'lū.
Sallumus, sal-lū'mus.
Salma, sal'mah.
Salmanasar, sal'man-ā''sàr.
Salmon, sal'mon.
Salmone, sal-mō'nē.
Salom, sā'lom.
Salome, sa-lō'mē.
Salu, sā'lū.
Salum, sā'lum.
Samael, sam'ā-el.
Samaias, sam-ī'as.
Samaria, sa-mā're-ah.
Samaritan, sa-mar'e-tan.
Samaritans, sa-mar'e-tanz.
Samatus, sam'a-tus.
Sameius, sam-ī'us.
Samgar-nebo, sam'gàr-nĕ''bō.
Sami, sā'mī.
Samis, sā'mis.
Samlah, sam'lah.
Samos, sā'mos.
Samothracia, sam'o-thrā''she-ah.
Sampsames, samp'sa-mēz.
Samson, sam'son.
Samuel, sam'ū-el.
Sanabassar, san'a-bas''sàr.
Sanabassarus, san'a-bas''sa-rus.
Sanasib, san'a-sib.
Sanballat, san-bal'lat.
Sansannah, san-san'nah.
Saph, saf.
Saphat, sā'fat.
Saphatias, saf'a-tī''as.
Sapheth, sā'feth.
Saphir, saf'ir.
Sapphira, saf-fī'rah.
Sara, } sa'rah.
Sarah, }
Sarai, sa-rā'ī, or sā'rī.
Sarabias, sar'a-bī''as.
Saraias, sa-rī'as.

Saramel, sar'a-mel.
Saraph, sā'raf.
Sarchedonus, sàr'kĕ'do-nus.
Sardeus, sàr-dĕ'us.
Sardis, sàr'dis.
Sardites, sàr'dīts.
Sarepta, sa-rep'tah.
Sargon, sàr'gon.
Sarid, sā'rid.
Sarmatia, sàr-mā'she-ah.
Saron, sā'ron.
Sarothie, sa-rō'the-ē.
Sarsechim, sàr'se-kim.
Saruch, sā'ruk.
Satan, sā'tan, or sat'an.
Sathrabuzanes,sath'ra-bū''za-nēz.
Saul, sawl.
Savaran, sav'a-ran.
Savias, sa-vī'as.
Scythin, sith'e-ah.
Scythian, sith'e-an.
Scythopolis, sī-thop'ō-lis.
Seba, sē'bah.
Sebat, sē'bat.
Secacah, sek'a-kah.
Sechenias, sek'eu-ī''as.
Sechu, sē'kū.
Secundus, se-kun'dus.
Sedecias, sed'e-sī''as.
Sceva, sē'vah.
Segub, sē'gub.
Seir, sē'ir.
Seirath, se-ī'rath.
Sela, } sē'lah.
Selah, }
Sela-Ham-Mahlekoth, sē'la-ham'ma-lē''koth.
Seled, sē'led.
Selemia, sel'e-mī''ah.
Selemias, sel'e-mī''as.
Seleucia, se-loo'she-ah, or sel'ū-sī''ah.
Seleucus, se-loo'kus.
Sem, sem.
Semachiah, sem'a-kī''ah.
Semei, sem'e-ī.
Semellius, sem'el-lī''us.
Senaah, sen'ā-ah.
Seneh, sē'nā.
Senir, sē'nir.
Sennacherib, sen-nak'e-rib.
Senuah, sen'ū-ah.
Seorim, sē'o-rim.
Sephar, sē'fàr.
Sepharad, sef'a-rad.
Sepharvaim, sef'àr-vā''im.

Sepharvites, sē'fär-vīts.
Serah, sē'rah.
Seraiah, ser-ī'ah.
Sered, sē'red.
Sergius Paulus, ser'je-us paw''lus.
Seron, sē'ron.
Serug, sē'rug.
Sesis, ses'is.
Sesthel, ses'thel.
Seth, seth.
Sethur, sē'thur.
Shaalabbin, shā-al'ab-bin.
Shaalbim, shā-al'bim, or shā'al-
bim.
Shaalbonite, shā-al'bō-nīt.
Shaaph, shā'af.
Shaaraim, shā'a-rā''im.
Shaashgaz, shā-ash'gaz.
Shabbethai, shab'be-tha''ī.
Shachia, sha-kī'ah.
Shaddai, shad-dā'ī.
Shadrach, shā'drak.
Shage, shā'gē.
Shaharaim, shā'ha-rā''im.
Shahazimah, shā-haz'e-mah.
Shalem, shā'lem.
Shalim, shā'lim.
Shalisha, shal'e-shah.
Shallecheth, shal'le-keth, or shal-
lek'eth.
Shallum, shal'lum.
Shallun, shal'lun.
Shalmai, shal-mā'ī.
Shalman, shal'man.
Shalmaneser, shal'ma-nē''zer.
Shama, shā'mah.
Shamariah, sham'a-rī''ah.
Shamed, shā'med.
Shamer, shā'mer.
Shamgar, sham'gär.
Shamhuth, sham'huth.
Shamir, shā'mir.
Shamma, } sham'mah.
Shammah,
Shammai, sham-mā'ī.
Shammoth, sham'moth.
Shammua, } sham-mū'ah.
Shammuah,
Shamsherai, sham'she-rā''ī.
Shapham, shā'fam.
Shaphan, shā'fan.
Shaphat, shā'fat.
Shapher, shā'fer.
Sharai, shar-ā'ī.
Sharaim, shar-ā'im.
Sharar, shā'rar.

Sharezer, sha-rē'zer.
Sharon, shā'ron.
Sharonite, shā'ron-īt.
Sharuhen, shar'ū-hen.
Shashai, sha-shā'ī.
Shashak, shā'shak.
Shaul, shā'ul.
Shaulites, shā'ul-īts.
Shaveh, shā'vā.
Shavsha, shav'shah.
Sheal, shē'al.
Shealtiel, she-al'te-el.
Sheariah, shē'a-rī''ah.
Shear-jashub, shē'är-jā''shub.
Sheba, } shē'bah.
Shebah,
Shebam, shē'bam.
Shebaniah, sheb'a-nī''ah.
Shebarim, sheb'a-rim.
Sheber, shē'ber.
Shebna, sheb'nah.
Shebuel, sheb'ū-el.
Shecaniah, } shek'a-nī''ah.
Shechaniah,
Shechem, shē'kem.
Shechemites, shē'kem-īts.
Shedeur, shed'e-ur.
Shehariah, shē'ha-rī''ah.
Shelah, shē'lah.
Shelanites, shē'lan-īts.
Shelemiah, shel'e-mī''ah.
Sheleph, shē'lef.
Shelesh, shē'lesh.
Shelomi, shel'o-mī.
Shelomith, shel'o-mith.
Shelomoth, shel'o-moth.
Shelumiel, she-lū'me-el.
Shem, shem.
Shema, shē'mah.
Shemaah, shem'ā-ah.
Shemaiah, shem-ī'ah.
Shemariah, shem'a-rī''ah.
Shemeber, shem'e-ber, or she-mē'-
ber.
Shemer, shē'mer.
Shemida, } shem'e-dah.
Shemidah,
Shemidaites, shem'e-dā''īts.
Sheminith, shem'e-nith.
Shemiramoth, she-mir'a-moth.
Shemuel, shem'ū-el.
Shen, shen.
Shenazar, shen'ā-zar.
Shenir, shē'nir.
Shepham, shē'fam.
Shephathiah, shef'a-thī''ah.

Shephatiah, shef'a-tī"ah.
Shephi, shē'fī.
Shepho, shē'fō.
Shephuphan, shef'ū-fan.
Sherah, shē'rah.
Sherebiah, sher'e-bī"ah.
Sheresh, shē'resh.
Sherezer, shē-rē'zer.
Sheshach, shē'shak.
Sheshai, shē-shā'ī.
Sheshan, shē'shan.
Sheshbazzar, shesh-baz'zàr.
Sheth, sheth.
Shethar, shē'thar.
Shethar-Boznai,   shē'thàr-boz-
  nā"ī.
Sheva, shē'vah.
Shibboleth, shib'bo-leth.
Shibmah, shib'mah.
Shicron, shī'kron.
Shiggaion, shig-gī'on.
Shigionoth, she-gī'o-noth.
Shihon, shī'hon.
Shihor, shī'hor.
Shihor-libnath, shī'hor-lib"nath.
Shilhi, shil'hī.
Shilhim, shil'him.
Shillem, shil'lem.
Shillemites, shil'lem-īts.
Shiloah, shī-lō'ah.
Shiloh, shī'lō.
Shiloni, shī-lō'nī.
Shilonite, shī'lon-īt.
Shilonites, shī'lon-īts.
Shilshah, shil'shah.
Shimea, } shim'e-ah.
Shimeah, }
Shimeam, shim'e-am.
Shimeath, shim'e-ath.
Shimeathites, shim'e-ath-īts.
Shimei, shim'e-ī.
Shimeon, shim'e-on.
Shimhi, shim'hī.
Shimi, shī'mī.
Shimites, shim'īts.
Shimma, shim'mah.
Shimon, shī'mon.
Shimrath, shim'rath.
Shimri, shim'rī.
Shimrith, shim'rith.
Shimron, shim'ron.
Shimronites, shim'ron-īts.
Shimron-meron,   shim'ron-mē"-
  ron.
Shimshai, shim-shā'ī.
Shinab, shī'nab.

Shinar, shī'nàr.
Shiphi, shif'ī.
Shiphmite, shif'mīt.
Shiphrah, shif'rah.
Shiphtan, shif'tan.
Shisha, shī'shah.
Shishak, shī'shak.
Shitrai, she-trā'ī.
Shittim, shit'tim.
Shiza, shī'zah.
Shoa, shō'ah.
Shobab, shō'bab.
Shobach, shō'bak.
Shobai, shō-bā'ī.
Shobal, shō'bal.
Shobek, shō'bek.
Shobi, shō-bī.
Shocho, } shō'kō.
Shochoh, }
Shoham, shō'ham.
Shomer, shō'mer.
Shophach, shō'fak.
Shophan, shō'fan.
Shoshannim, sho-shan'nim.
Shoshannimeduth, sho-shan'nim-
  ē"duth.
Shua, } shoo'ah.
Shuah, }
Shual, shoo'al.
Shubael, shoo'bā-el.
Shuham, shoo'ham.
Shuhamites, shoo'ham-īts.
Shuhite, shoo'hīt.
Shulamite, shoo'lam-īt.
Shumathites, shoo'math-īts.
Shunammite, shoo'nam-mīt.
Shunem, shoo'nem.
Shuni, shoo'nī.
Shunites, shoo'nīts.
Shuphamites, shoo'fam-īts.
Shuppim, shup'pim.
Shur, shur.
Shushan, shoo'shan.
Shushan-eduth, shoo'shan-ē"duth.
Shuthalhites, shoo'thal-hīts.
Shuthelah, shoo'the-lah, or shoo-
  thē'lah.
Sia, sī'ah.
Siaha, sī'a-hah.
Sibbecai. } sib'be-kā"ī.
Sibbechai, }
Sibboleth, sib'bo-leth.
Sibmah, sib'mah.
Sibraim, sib-rā'im.
Sichem, sī'kem.
Sicyon, sis'e-on.

Siddim, sid'dim.
Side, sī'dē.
Sidon, sī'don.
Sidonians, sī-dō'ne-anz.
Sihon, sī'hon.
Sihor, sī'hor.
Silas, sī'las.
Silla, sil'lah.
Siloah, se-lō'ah.
Siloam, sī-lō'am.
Silvanus, sil-vā'nus.
Simalcue, sim'al-kū"ē.
Simeon, sim'e-on.
Simeonites, sim'e-on-īts.
Simon, sī'mon.
Simon Bar-jona, sī'mon bàr-jō"-nah.
Simon Chosamæus, sī'mon kos'a-mē"us.
Simon Peter, sī'mon pē"tr.
Simri, sim'rī.
Sin, sin.
Sina, sī'nah.
Sinai, sī'nī.
Sinite, sī'nīt.
Sinon, sin'on.
Sion, zī'on.
Siphmoth, sif'moth.
Sippai, sip-pā'ī.
Sirach, sī'rak.
Sirah, sī'rah.
Sirion, sir'e-on.
Sisamai, ses'a-mā"ī.
Sisera, sis'e-rah.
Sisinnes, se-sin'nēz.
Sitnah, sit'nah.
Sivan, sī'van.
Smyrna, smer'nah.
So, sō.
Socho, } sō'kō.
Sochoh, }
Socoh, sō'kō.
Sodi, sō'dī.
Sodom, sod'om.
Sodomite, sod'om-īt.
Sodomites, sod'om-īts.
Sodoma. sod'o-mah.
Sodomitish, sod'om-īt"ish.
Solomon, sol'o-mon.
Sopater, sō'pa-ter.
Sophereth, sof'e-reth.
Sophonias, sof'on-ī"as.
Sorek, sō'rek.
Sosipater, sō-sip'a-ter.
Sosthenes, sos'the-nēz.
Sostratus, sos'trā-tus.

Sotai, sō-tā'ī.
Spain, spàn.
Sparta, spàr'tah.
Stachys, stā'kis.
Stephanas, stef'a-nas.
Stephen, stē'vn.
Stoicks, stō'iks.
Suah, sū'ah.
Suba, sū'bah.
Subai, su-bā'ī.
Succoth, suk'koth.
Succoth-Benoth, suk'koth-bē"-noth.
Suchathites, sū'kath-īts.
Sud, sud.
Sudias, sū'de-as.
Sukkiims, suk'ke-imz.
Sur, sur.
Susanchites, soo'san-kīts.
Susanna, soo-zan'nah.
Susi, soo'sī.
Susiana, soo'sī-ā"nah.
Sychar, sī'kàr.
Sychem, sī'kem.
Sychemite, sī'kem-īt.
Syelus, sī-ē'lus.
Syene, sī-ē'ne.
Syntyche, sin'te-ke.
Syracuse, sir'a-kus.
Syria, sir'e-ah.
Syriac, sir'e-ak.
Syriau, sir'e-an.
Syrians, sir'e-anz.
Syria-Damascus, sir'e-ah-da-mas"kus.
Syria-maachah, sir'e-ah-mā"a-kah.
Syrophenicia, sī'rō-fe-nish"e-ah.
Syrophenician, sī'rō-fe-nish"e-an.

Taanach, tā'a-nak.
Taanath-Shiloh, tā'a-nath-shī"lō.
Tabbaoth, tab'bā-oth.
Tabbath, tab'bath.
Tabeal, tā'bē-al.
Tabeel, tā'be-el.
Tabellius, ta-bel'le-us.
Taberah, tab'e-rah.
Tabitha, tab'e-thah.
Tabor, tā'bor.
Tabrimon, tab're-mon.
Tachmonite, tak'mon-īt.
Tadmor, tad'mor.
Tahan, tā'han.
Tahanites, tā'han-īts.
Tahapanes, ta-hap'a-nēz.

Tahath, tä'hath.
Tahpanhes, täh'pan-hēz.
Tahpenes, täh'pe-nēz.
Tahrea, täh'rē-ah.
Tahtim–hodshi, täh'tim-hod''she.
Talitha–cumi, tal-ĭ'tha-kū''mĭ.
Talmai, tal-mā'ĭ.
Talmon, tal'mon.
Talsas, tal'sas.
Tamah, tā'mah.
Tamar, tā'mar.
Tammuz, tam'muz.
Tanach, tā'nak.
Tanhumeth, tan-hū'meth.
Tanis, tā'nis.
Taphath, tā'fath.
Taphon, tā'fon.
Tappuah, tap-pū'ah.
Tarah, tā'rah.
Taralah, tar'a-lah.
Tarea, tā-rē'ah.
Tarpelites, tär'pel-īts.
Tarshish, tär'shish.
Tarsus, tär'sus.
Tartak, tär'tak.
Tartan, tär'tan.
Tatnai, tat-nā'ĭ.
Tebah, tē'bah.
Tebaliah, teb'a-lī''ah.
Tebeth, tē'beth.
Tehaphnehes, te-haf'ne-hēz.
Tehinnah, te-hin'nah.
Tekel, tē'kel.
Tekoa, } te-kō'ah.
Tekoah, }
Tekoite, te-kō'īt.
Tekoites, te-kō'īts.
Telabib, tel-ā'bib.
Telah, tē'lah.
Telaim, tel'ā-im.
Telassar, te-las'sar.
Telem, tē'lem.
Telharesha, tel-har'e-shah.
Telharsa, tel-här'sah.
Telmelah, tel-mē'lah.
Tema, tē'mah.
Teman, tē'man.
Temanite, tē'man-īt.
Temanites, tē'man-īts.
Temani, tē'ma-nī.
Temeni, tē'men-ī.
Terah, tē'rah.
Teresh, tē'rish.
Tertius, ter'she-us.
Tertullus, ter-tul'lus.
Teta, tē'tah.

Thaddeus, thad'dē-us.
Thahash, thā'hash.
Thamah, thā'mah.
Thamar, thā'mar.
Thamnatha, tham'na-thah.
Thara, thā'rah.
Tharra, thar'rah.
Tharshish, thär'shish.
Tharsus, thär'sus.
Thassi, thas'sĭ.
Thebes, thēbz.
Thebez, thē'bēz.
Thecoe, the-kō'ē.
Thelasar, thel'a-sar.
Thelersas, the-ler'sas.
Theman, thē'man.
Theocanus, thē'ō-kā''nus.
Theodotus, the-od'o-tus.
Theophilus, the-of'e-lus.
Theras, thē'ras.
Thermeleth, ther'me-leth.
Thessalonians, thes'sa-lō''ne-anz.
Thessalonica, thes'sa-lo-nī''kah.
Theudas, thū'das.
Thimnathah, thim'na-thah, or
thim-nā'thah.
Thisbe, this'bē.
Thomas, tom'as.
Thomoi, tho mō'ĭ.
Thracia, thrā'she-ah.
Thraseas, thra-sē'as.
Thummim, thum'mim.
Thyatira, thī'a-tī''rah.
Tiberias, tī-bē're-as.
Tiberius Cæsar, tī-bē're-us sē''zar.
Tibhath, tib'hath.
Tibni, tib'nĭ.
Tidal, tī'dal.
Tiglath–pileser, tig'lath-pe-lē''-
zer.
Tigris, tī'gris.
Tikvah, tik'vah.
Tikvath, tik'vath.
Tilgath–pilneser, til'gath-pil-nē''-
zer.
Tilon, tī'lon.
Timeus, tī-mē'us.
Timna, } tim'nah.
Timnah, }
Timnath, tim'nath.
Timnath–Heres, tim'nath-hē''rēz.
Timnath–Serah, tim'nath-sē''rah.
Timnite, tim'nīt.
Timon, tī'mon.
Timotheus, te-mō'the-us.
Timothy, tim'o-the.

Tiphsah, tif'sah.
Tiras, ti'ras.
Tirathites, ti'rath-its.
Tirhakah, tir'ha-kah.
Tirhanah, tir'ha-nah.
Tiria, tir'e-ah.
Tirshatha, tir'sha-thah, or tir-shā'-thah.
Tirza, } tir'zah.
Tirzah, }
Tishbite, tish'bit.
Titans, ti'tanz.
Titus, ti'tus.
Tizite, ti'zit.
Toah, tō'ah.
Tob, tob.
Tob-Adonijah, tob-ad'o-ni''jah.
Tobiah, tō-bī'ah.
Tobias, tō-bī'as.
Tobie, tō-bī'ē.
Tobiel, tō-bī'el.
Tobijah, to-bī'jah.
Tobit, to'bit.
Tochen, tō'ken.
Togarmah, to-gär'mah.
Tohu, tō'hū.
Toi, tō i.
Tola, tō'lah.
Tolai es, tō'lā-its.
Tolad, tō'lad.
Tolbanes, tol'ba-nēz.
Tophel, tō'fel.
Tophet, tō'fet.
Topheth, tō'feth.
Tou, tō'ū.
Trachonitis, trak'o-ni''tis.
Tripolis, trip'o-lis.
Troas, trō'as.
Trogyllium, trō-jil'le-um.
Trophimus, trof'e-mus.
Tryphena, tri-fē'nah.
Tryphon, tri'fon.
Tryphosa, tri-fō'sah.
Tubal, tū'bal.
Tubal-cain, tū'bal-kān.
Tubieni, tū'be-ē''ni.
Tychicus, ti'ke-kus.
Tyrannus, ti-ran'nus.
Tyre, tir.
Tyrians, tir'ē-anz.
Tyrus, ti'rus.

Ucal, ū'kal.
Uel, ū'el.
Ulai, ū-lā'i.
Ulam, ū'lam.

Ulla, ul'lah.
Ummah, um'mah.
Unni, un'ni.
Upharsin, ū-fär'sin.
Uphaz, ū'faz.
Ur, ur.
Urbane, ur'ban.
Uri, ū'ri.
Uriah, ū-rī'ah.
Urias, ū-rī'as.
Uriel, ū're-el.
Urijah, ū-rī'jah.
Urim, ū'rim.
Uthai, ū-thā'ī.
Uthii, ū'the-ī.
Uz, uz.
Uzai, ū zā'ī.
Uzal, ū'zal.
Uzza, } uz'zah.
Uzzah, }
Uzzen-sherah, uz'zen-shē''rah.
Uzzi, uz'zi.
Uzzia, } uz zī'ah.
Uzziah, }
Uzziel, uz'ze-el.
Uzzielites, uz'ze-el-īts.

Vajezatha, va-jez-ā'thah.
Vaniah, va-nī'ah.
Vashni, vash'ni.
Vashti, vash'tī.
Vophsi, vof'sī.

Zaanan, zā'a-nan.
Zaananuim, zā'a-nan''nim.
Zaavan, zā'a-van.
Zabad, zā'bad.
Zabadaias, zab'a-dī''as.
Zabadeus, zab'a-dē''anz.
Zabbai, zab-bā'ī.
Zabbud, zab'bud.
Zabdeus, zab-dē'us.
Zabdi, zab'dī.
Zabdiel, zab'de-el.
Zabud, zā'bud.
Zabulon, zab'ū-lon.
Zaccai, zak-kā'ī.
Zaccheus, zak-kē'us.
Zacchur, } zak'kur.
Zaccur, }
Zachariah, zak'a-rī''ah.
Zacharias, zak'a-rī''as.
Zachary, zak'ar-e.
Zacher, zā'ker.
Zadok, zā'dok.
Zaham, zā'ham.

Zair, zā'ir.
Zalaph, zā'laf.
Zalmon, zal'mon.
Zalmonah, zal'mō-nah.
Zalmunna, zal'mun-nah.
Zambis, zam'bis.
Zambri, zam'brī.
Zamoth, zā'moth.
Zamzummims, zam'zum-mimz.
Zanoah, za-nō'ah.
Zaphnath-Paaneah, zaf'nath-pā'a-nē"ah.
Zaphon, zā'fon.
Zara, } zā'rah.
Zarah, }
Zaraces, zar'a-sēz.
Zaraias, za-rī'as.
Zareah, zā'rē-ah.
Zareathites, zā'rē-ath-īts.
Zared, zā'red.
Zarephath, zăr'e-fath.
Zaretan, zăr'e-tan.
Zareth-Shahar, zā'reth-shā"har.
Zarhites, zăr'hīts.
Zartanah, zăr'ta-nah.
Zarthan, zăr'than.
Zathoe, zath'o-ē.
Zathui, zath'ū-ī.
Zatthu, zat'thū.
Zattu, zat'tū.
Zavan, zā'van.
Zaza, zā'zah.
Zebadiah, zeb'a-dī"ah.
Zebah, zē'bah.
Zebaim, ze-bā'im, or zē'bā-im.
Zebedee, zeb'e-dē.
Zebina, zeb'e-inah.
Zeboiim, ze-boy'im.
Zeboim, zē'bō-im.
Zebudah, zeb'ū-dah.
Zebul, zē'bul.
Zebulon, zeb'ū-lon.
Zebulonite, zeb'ū-lon-īt.
Zebulonites, zeb'ū-lon-īts.
Zebulun, zeb'ū-lun.
Zechariah, zek'a-rī"ah.
Zedad, zē'dad, or zē-dad'.
Zedekiah, zed'e-kī"ah.
Zedekias, zed'e-kī"as.
Zeeb, zē'eb.
Zelah, zē'lah.
Zelek, zē'lek.
Zelophehad, ze-lō'fe-had.
Zelotes, ze-lō'tēz.
Zelzah, zel'zah.
Zemaraim, zem'a-rā"im.

Zemarite, zem'a-rīt.
Zemira, ze-mī'rah, or zem'ī-rah.
Zenan, zē'nan, or zē nan'.
Zenas, zē'nas.
Zephaniah, zef'a-nī"ah.
Zephath, zē'fath.
Zephathah, zef'a-thah.
Zephi, zē'fī.
Zepho, zē'fō.
Zephon, zē'fon.
Zephonites, zē'fon-īts.
Zephyrus, zef'e-rus.
Zer, zer.
Zerah, zē'rah.
Zerahiah, zer'a-hī"ah.
Zered, zē'red.
Zereda, zer'e-dah.
Zeredathah, zē-red'a-thah.
Zererath, zer'e-rath.
Zeresh, zē'resh.
Zereth, zē'reth.
Zeri, zē'rī.
Zeror, zē'ror.
Zeruah, ze-roo'ah, or zer'ū-ah.
Zerubbabel, ze-rub'ba-bel.
Zeruiah, zer'ū-ī"ah.
Zetham, zē'tham.
Zethan, zē'than.
Zethar, zē'thăr.
Zia, zī'ah.
Ziba, zī'bah.
Zibeon, zib'e-on.
Zibia, } zib'e-ah.
Zibiah, }
Zichri, zik'rī.
Ziddim, zid'dim.
Zidkijah, zid-kī'jah.
Zidon, zī'don.
Zidonians, zī dō'ne-anz.
Zif, zif.
Ziha, zī'hah.
Ziklag, zik'lag.
Zilla, zil'lah.
Zilpah, zil'pah.
Zilthai, zil-thā'ī.
Zimmah, zim'mah.
Zimran, zim'ran.
Zimri, zim'rī.
Zin, zin.
Zina, zī'nah.
Zion, zī'on.
Zior, zī'or.
Ziph, zif.
Ziphah, zī'fah.
Ziphims, zif'imz.
Ziphion, zif'e-on.

Ziphites, zif'its.
Ziphron, zif'ron.
Zippor, zip'por.
Zipporah, zip-pō'rah, or zip'pō-rah.
Zithri, zith'rī.
Ziz, ziz.
Ziza, } zī'zah.
Zizah, }
Zoan, zō'an.
Zoar, zō'ăr.
Zoba, } zō'bah.
Zobah, }
Zobebah, zō'be-bah.
• Zohar, zō'hăr.
Zoheleth, zō'hē-leth.
Zoheth, zō'heth.

Zophah, zō'fah.
Zophai, zō-fā'ī.
Zophar, zō'făr.
Zophim, zō'fim.
Zorah, zō'rah.
Zorathites, zō'rath-īts.
Zoreah, zō're-ah.
Zorites, zō'rīts.
Zorobabel, zo-rob'a-bel.
Zuar, zū'ar.
Zuph, zuf.
Zur, zur.
Zuriel, zu're-el.
Zuri-Shaddai, zū'rī-shad-dā'ī.
Zuzims, zū'zimz.

ORIGIN OF NATIONS.—NOAH'S SONS—SHEM, HAM, AND JAPHETH.

Gen. x.—JAPHETH'S SONS.*

Sons of Japheth.	Principal Countries peopled by them.	Principal Nations sprung from them.
	Asia Minor, Armenia, Caucasus, Europe.	
Gomer . .	. . . .	Russians, Germans, Gauls, Britons.
Magog . .	. . . .	Scythians.
Madai . .	. . . .	Medes.—So Josephus.
Javan . .	. . . .	Ionians and Athenians.
Tubal . .	. . . .	Iberians.—Josephus. And Albanians.
Meshech .	. . . .	Moscovites.
Tiras . .	. . . .	Thracians, or the People of the Hellespont, now called the Dardanelles.

SHEM'S SONS.

Sons of Shem.	Principal Countries peopled by them.	Principal Nations sprung from them.
	Assyria, Syria, Persia, Arabia, N. Mesopotamia.	
Elam . .	. . . .	Elamites, or Persians.
Asshur . .	. . . .	Assyrians. [sephus.
Arphaxad .	. . . .	"Chaldeans are Arphaxadeans."—Jo-
Lud . . .	. . . .	Lydians.—So Bishop Watson.
Aram . .	. . . .	Syrians, Armenians.

HAM'S SONS.

Sons of Ham.	Principal Countries peopled by them.	Principal Nations sprung from them.
	Arabia, Egypt, North Coast of Africa.	
Cush . .	. . . .	Ethiopians, or Abyssinians.
Misraim .	. . . .	Egyptians.
Phut . .	. . . .	Lybians.
Canaan . .	. . . .	Canaanites.

* Gen. x. 5. "By these were the *isles*," etc. The word translated isles rather means *countries*, especially those washed by the sea.

THE JEWISH YEAR.

Month of Sacred Year.	Civil Year.	Name.	Number of days.	English Months.	Products.	Jewish Festivals.
I.	VII.	Abib, or Nisan (Exod. xii. 2; xiii. 4).	30	Mar., Apr.	Barley ripe. Fig in blossom.	Passover. Unleavened Bread.
II.	VIII.	Jyar, or Zif.	29	April and May.	Barley harvest.	
III.	IX.	Sisan, or Sivan.	30	May and June.	Wheat harvest.	Pentecost.
IV.	X.	Thammuz.	29	June, Jul.	Early vintage.	
V.	XI.	Ab (Ezra vii. 9).	30	July, Aug.	Ripe figs.	
VI.	XII.	Elul (Neh. vi. 15).	29	Aug., Sep.	General vintage.	Feast of Trumpets.
VII.	I.	Tizri (1 Kings viii. 2).	30	Sep., Oct.	Ploughing and Sowing.	Atonement. Feast of Tabernacles.
VIII.	II.	Bul (1 Kings vi. 38).	29	Oct., Nov.	Latter grapes.	
IX.	III.	Chisleu (Zech. vii. 1).	30	Nov., Dec.	Snow.	Dedication.
X.	IV.	Thebeth (Esth. ii. 16).	29	Dec., Jan.	Grass after rain.	
XI.	V.	Shebat (Zech. i. 7).	30	Jan., Feb.	Winter fig.	
XII.	VI.	Adar (Ezra vi. 15).	29	Feb., Mar.	Almond Blossom.	Purim.
XIII.		Ve-Adar, Intercalary.				

N. B.—The Sacred year was reckoned from the moon after the vernal equinox.

The Civil year began in September (the fruitless part of the year). The prophets speak of the *sacred* year; those engaged in secular pursuits, of the *civil* year. The year was divided into 12 *lunar* months, with a thirteenth, or *intercalary* month, every third year.

BIBLE TIME.

The *Natural* Day was from sunrise to sunset.
The *Natural* Night was from sunset to sunrise.
The *Civil* Day was from sunset one evening to sunset the next; for, "the Evening and the Morning were the first day."

Night (Ancient).
First Watch (Lam. ii. 19) till midnight.
Middle Watch (Judg. vii. 19) till 3 A. M.
Morning Watch (Exod. xiv. 24) till 6 A. M.

Night (New Testament).
First Watch, *evening,* = 6 to 9 P. M.

Second Watch, *midnight,* = 9 to 12 P. M.
Third Watch, *cock-crow,* = 12 to 3 A. M.
Fourth Watch, *morning,* = 3 to 6 A. M.

Day (Ancient).
Morning till about 10 A. M.
Heat of day till about 2 P. M.
Cool of day till about 6 P. M.

Day (New Testament).

Third hour = 6 to 9 A. M.
Sixth hour = 9 to 12 midday.

Ninth hour = 12 to 3 P. M.
Twelfth hour = 3 to 6 P. M.

N. B.—Our Lord's prediction of his resurrection is in accordance with the usual expressions respecting the *civil*, not the *natural* day : thus, "three days and three nights" is, in the Greek, all one word, which would be more correctly translated, "three civil days;" implying that each consisted of twenty-four hours, and that the intervening *nights* were included, and that he did not mean he should be in the grave by *day* and *not* by *night*.

"SEEK, AND YE SHALL FIND."

Blest they who seek,
While in their youth,
With spirit meek,
The way of truth.
To them the sacred Scriptures now display
Christ as the only true and living way!
His precious blood on Calvary was given,
To make them heirs of endless life in heaven;
And e'en on earth the child of God can trace
The glorious blessings of his Saviour's grace!
For them He bore
His Father's frown;
For them He wore
The thorny crown;
Nailed to the cross,
Endured its pain,
That His life's loss
Might be their gain;
Then haste to choose
That better part,
Nor dare refuse
The Lord thy heart,
Lest He declare
"I know you not;"
And deep despair
Shall be your lot!
With Jesus plead—
Christ crucified;—
He'll help your need;
For you He died.